Don't let those language skills get lost or rusty!

As a teacher you work hard to teach language skills to your students. Your students work hard to master them. Do you worry that your students will forget the material as you move on to the next concept?

If so, here's a plan for you and your students—one that will keep those skills sharp.

Use It! Don't Lose It! provides daily language practice for all the basic skills. There are five language problems a day, every day for 36 weeks. The skills are correlated to national and state standards.

Students practice all the ninth-grade skills, concepts, and processes in a spiraling sequence. The plan starts with the basic level of ninth-grade skills, progressing gradually to higher-level tasks, as it continually circles around and back to the same skills at a little higher level, again and again. Each time a skill shows up, it has a new context—requiring students to dig into their memories, recall what they know, and apply it to another situation.

The Weekly Plan — Five Problems a Day for 36 Weeks

Monday – Thursday ....
- one vocabulary or other word skills item
- one spelling or mechanics item (capitalization, punctuation)
- one grammar or language usage item

Monday and **Wednesday** ....
- one reading item
- one literature item

Tuesday and **Thursday** ....
- one writing item
- one research/information skills item

Friday ....
- one longer reading comprehension passage with questions
- one writing task

Contents

How to Use Daily Skills Practice

To get started, reproduce each page, slice the Monday–Thursday lesson pages in half or prepare a transparency. The lessons can be used . . .

- **for independent practice**—Reproduce the lessons and let students work individually or in pairs to practice skills at the beginning or end of a language class.
- **for small group work**—Students can discuss and solve the problems together and agree on answers.
- **for the whole class review**—Make a transparency and work through the problems together as a class.

Helpful Hints for Getting Started

- Though students may work alone on the items, always find a way to review and discuss the answers together. In each review, ask students to describe how they solved the problem-solving problems or other problems that involve choices of strategies.

- Allow more time for the Friday lesson, as these tasks may take a little longer. Students can work in small groups to discover and discuss their answers.

- Provide dictionaries and other resources that may be helpful to students as needed. There will not always be room on the sheet for some of the longer writing tasks.

- Many of the writing tasks can be expanded into full writing lessons. When you have time to do so, extend the activity to work on all or various stages of the writing process. Find time for students to share and enjoy their written products.

- The daily lessons are designed to be completed in a short time period, so that they can be used along with your regular daily instruction. However, don't end the discussion until you are sure all students "get it," or at least until you know which ones don't get something and will need extra instruction. This will strengthen all the other work students do in language class.

- Keep a consistent focus on thinking skills for reading comprehension activities. Allow students to discuss their answers, particularly those that involve higher-level thinking skills such as drawing conclusions, inferring, predicting, or evaluating.

- Find ways to strengthen the knowledge and use of new vocabulary words students learn in the daily practice. Keep a running list of these words. Use them in classroom discussions and activities. Find ways to share and show off knowledge of the words. Encourage students to include the new words in their writing.

- Take note of which items leave some or all of the students confused or uncertain. This will alert you to which skills need more instruction.

- The daily lessons may include some topics or skills your students have not yet learned. In these cases, students may skip items. Or, you might encourage them to consider how the problem could be solved. Or, you might use the occasion for a short lesson that would get them started on this skill.

Use It! Don't Lose It!

LANGUAGE
Daily Skills Practice
Grade 9

by Amy Carlon and Jill Norris

IncentivePublications

Illustrated by Kathleen Bullock
Cover by Geoffrey Brittingham
Copyedited by Stephanie McGuirk

ISBN 978-0-86530-654-7

5   6   7   8   9   10   14   13   12   11

Printed by Sheridan Books, Inc., Chelsea, Michigan • October 2011
www.incentivepublications.com

MONDAY WEEK 1 _Sage_
Name

1. Circle the letters that should be capitalized.

(a)pollo, (a)thena, and (p)oseidon are a few of the familiar gods and goddesses associated with greek mythology; but (z)eus was the god held in highest regard by the ancient greeks.

2. What is the meaning of the underlined word?

Odysseus, who built a giant hollow horse so that he and his men could surprise the Trojans, used his clever <u>tactics</u> to win the Trojan War.

3. Which sentence is a compound sentence?

(a) The Greeks and Romans believed in gods and goddesses.

b. The Sirens were renowned for their beautiful singing; however, their songs lured many sailors to their demise.

4. Circle the synonyms for **abdicate**.

(resign) seize usurp cede (relinquish)

5. Read the passage below. Write a sentence to summarize the differences between a myth and a legend.

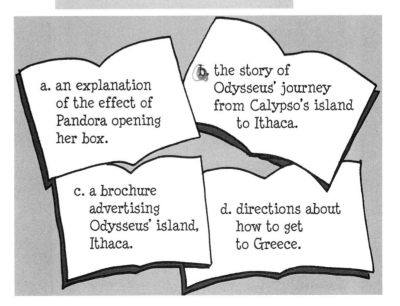

Although the difference between a myth and a legend is slight, there is a difference. A myth involves gods and goddesses and originates from archaic folklore. It attempts to explain the origin of life or some of the strange happenings that occur in the world. On the other hand, a legend involves human actions and is handed down from generation to generation. A legend may be considered true even though it is usually a mixture of fact and fiction.

TUESDAY WEEK 1 _Sage_
Name

1. Choose the term that best describes the statement.

I've got my eye on you!

○ cliché   ○ jargon   ⦿ idiom

2. Which sentence uses **riding** as a verb?

a. Odysseus, riding inside the massive horse, was able to hide himself well.

b. I think riding on Pegasus would be exhilarating.

c. All the gods were riding white horses.

3. Choose the best word for the sentence.

The gods and goddesses were _____ when the mortals did not do as they asked.

○ begrudged   ○ amused   ⦿ enraged

4. Circle the prefixes that mean **against**.

(contradict)   (antiwar)   (expel)
(postpone)   (oppose)   suffice

5. Which is an example of narrative writing?

a. an explanation of the effect of Pandora opening her box.

(b.) the story of Odysseus' journey from Calypso's island to Ithaca.

c. a brochure advertising Odysseus' island, Ithaca.

d. directions about how to get to Greece.

1. Write three definitions of the word **hit**. Include one definition that is traditional and two that have evolved in recent years.

2. Add correct punctuation to the passage. Indicate words that should be capitalized.

> **the most powerful greek gods lived atop mount olympus there on the mountaintop the gods renewed their immortality watched the games of mortal men and discussed their concerns**

3. Circle the correctly spelled words.

peice calender fiery foreign guarantee

4. What kind of mood does this sentence convey?

> The black night, a carefully knitted blanket shielding against all threatened dangers, protected the men as they began their journey.

5. Paraphrase the passage below.

> Poseidon, the god of water, was angry with his brother Zeus for exiling him from Mount Olympus. Poseidon flooded the land to kill the people who held Zeus in high esteem. As Poseidon unleashed the waters, Zeus heard his people cry and called upon Hephaestus, the god of fire, to help. Hephaestus designed a three-dimensional cone. He placed molten rock inside the cone.
>
> Zeus squeezed the cone, and it spewed forth liquid rock. The rock cooled quickly in the water and made land for Zeus' people. Zeus named this contraption a volcano.

1. Change the nouns to make them possessive.

Pegasus

Athena and Medusa

horse

2. Circle the abstract nouns.

sword   love   chariot   monster

wisdom   sandal   courage   map

3. Which sentence uses **farther** correctly?

- Odysseus traveled farther than anyone else to get to Ithaca.
- Zeus' power was farther advanced than Hera's.

4. Choose the reference you would use to locate Athens, Greece.

○ dictionary   atlas ○ almanac

5. Write three gerund phrases that describe the journey of Helios, the sun, as he galloped across the sky.

Read

1. List six adjectives that describe Atalanta. Use specific words. For example, was she *retiring* or *assertive, resourceful* or *dependent?*

2. List six adjectives that describe Hippomenes.

When Atalanta was born, she was taken into the woods and left to die. Saved by a mother bear, the tiny girl grew up with cubs as siblings. Years later, a band of hunters found Atalanta living in the bear's cave. The astonished men claimed her and taught her all the skills of the hunt. Each of the hunters viewed her as his own daughter. By the time she was a teenager, Atalanta was more skillful with a bow and arrow than any of her fathers.

She proved her skill on one hunt when two malicious centaurs confronted her. These half-human, half-horse beasts laughed at the sight of the young girl alone in the forest. They charged into the clearing where she stood. Fearlessly Atalanta faced their thundering hooves. She calmly fitted a bronze-tipped arrow to her bow and shot it. While the first arrow was in the air, she quickly aimed and fired a second one. Then she turned and walked away. The two centaurs lay motionless behind her, each with an arrow through its heart.

Not only was Atalanta a beautiful and skilled huntress, she was also the fastest runner of all humans. News of her skill and her speed spread throughout Greece. Her true parents came forward and her father urged her to marry. Atalanta did not want to give up the freedom she enjoyed in the woods. She consented to marry only if her suitor could defeat her in a footrace. Many men challenged her, but they all failed to outpace the stunning huntress.

One young man, Hippomenes, watched in awe as Atalanta won race after race. She was as swift and graceful as a falcon. Her dark hair rippled over her white shoulders, the colored ribbons she wore fluttered in the air, and her face grew dewy pink as she ran. Hippomenes fell deeply in love. He wanted to marry Atalanta, but he knew that he could never defeat her in a footrace.

Hippomenes prayed to Aphrodite, goddess of love, to help him win Atalanta's favor. Aphrodite answered his prayer and gave him three gleaming, golden apples. Hippomenes challenged Atalanta to a race. Atalanta admired the handsome warrior and considered letting him win the race. But as the race began, she exploded quietly into the lead. Hippomenes threw a gleaming apple to the side of the path. Atalanta stooped to retrieve it and Hippomenes pulled ahead. Twice more Hippomenes threw a sparkling treasure and caused Atalanta to slow her pace. The delay cost her the race. Hippomenes crossed the finish line just in front of Atalanta and won the right to marry her.

And so the two were married, and Atalanta fell in love with her handsome partner. The pair spent their days oblivious to the cares of the world around them. Sadly, the young lovers' happiness was short-lived. Aphrodite, who expected tributes of gratitude from Hippomenes, decided to punish him by changing the pair into lions and yoking them to a chariot.

Write

Write a persuasive paragraph to support or disagree with the premise.

> **Ultimately, Atalanta was the winner of the footrace even though Hippomenes crossed the finish line first.**

1. Circle the words that are antonyms for **dissent**.

(agree) oppose   concur

rebel   (consent)   differ

2. Circle the relative pronouns

that   (anyone)   (who) he

(she)   which   (all)   (whom)

3. Indicate the words that need to be capitalized.

in 2002, 38,000 people took part in (la) (tomatina,) (the) largest food fight festival ever. at the festival participants threw over 120 tons of tomatoes.

4. Write the plural of each noun.

asparagus	squash	potato
raspberry	celery	bacon strip
shrimp	escargot	grapefruit

5. Underline the topic sentence. Number each detail that supports it.

Health authorities cite many reasons for maintaining a healthy, well-balanced diet. Eating the right foods increases energy. Individuals with well-balanced diets excel in sports and academics. Statistics show that when people eat healthy, they have a reduced occurrence of heart disease and cancer, and as a result live longer. Eating a healthy, well-balanced diet is one important step to living a long, healthy life.

1. Choose the correct word for the sentence.

Doctors _____ people to eat vegetables and nuts that have unsaturated fat.

⊗ advise   ○ advice

2. Which statement represents an opinion?

(a.) Eating high-calorie, saturated fat increases the chance of heart attacks.

b. If people eat fattening foods, it is their own fault if they gain weight.

3. Underline the subordinate clause.

Peanuts, also used in the manufacturing of dynamite, are a good source of protein.

4. Identify the case of each pronoun.

whom _____   their _____

they _____   she _____

5. Combine the simple sentences to form a sequential paragraph. You may want to combine several of the sentences to improve the readability.

- Frankie gave Bobby some mouthwash.
- Bobby ate an onion-and-peanut-butter sandwich for breakfast.
- Frankie gagged at the smell of Bobby's breath.
- Bobby doesn't eat onion-and-peanut-butter sandwiches anymore.
- Bobby went to school without brushing his teeth.
- Bobby greeted Frankie with a friendly, "Hi, Buddy!"

Onion & Peanut Butter

Hold for Bobby

1. Name the type of poetry.

There once was a cook with a spoon
Who stirred by the light of the moon.
Her crumpets were sweet.
They couldn't be beat.
What dish will she make come high noon?

2. Write a topic sentence for a paragraph that discusses a nutritious school lunch program.

3. Add quotation marks to the passage below.

Do you know how long the longest banana split was? asked Jeff. The people of Selinsgrove, Pennsylvania, do. They made a banana split that was 4.55 miles long.

4. What is the meaning of this statement?

I am so hungry I could eat a horse!

5. Replace the incorrectly-used words on the sign.

Stuffed Cafe
Features of the Day

● Succulent seefood covered in a tangy mustered soss —It will leave you wanting just one more byte!

● Mouth-watering stakes grilled to perfection —A treat for your taste buds!

● Delectable deserts —Shore to enhance your dinning experience!

Begin you're amazing evening hear.

1. Write two meanings of the verb **mull**.

_____   _____

2. Choose the literary element used in the sentence.

Susan suddenly sensed the sublime aroma of warm chocolate.

○ simile
○ onomatopoeia
☑ alliteration

3. Choose the type of sentence.

Caramelizing onions takes lots of time and requires patience.

○ interrogative   ☑ declarative

4. Underline the direct object in the sentence.

Grandma's <u>fresh rolls</u> require room-temperature butter.

5. What is the main idea of the passage?

Can new brands compete with the original? In 1930 Ruth Wakefield made the very first chocolate chip cookie at the Toll House Inn in Whitman, Massachusetts. When she sold her recipe to Nestle, the chocolate company began to market semisweet chocolate morsels. Today you can buy dozens of different flavored cookie chips—raspberry, peanut butter, butterscotch, mint—as well as many varieties of chocolate chips. Recently taste-testers ranked the original chocolate morsels a respectable third in a comprehensive taste test.

Read

Read the paragraph about the breakfast casserole before answering the questions.

Grandma's Breakfast Casserole

Any crisp December Sunday at daybreak you'll find Grandma in the kitchen humming quietly as she fixes her special Maple Sausage and Waffle Casserole. She knows that a crowd will arrive hungry after early church services and she wants to be prepared. She browns the sausage, smothers the links in a bath of brown sugar mixed with maple syrup, and pops them into the oven. Then she combines the waffle mix, eggs, and milk, stirring just enough to moisten the dry ingredients. With one eye on the waffle iron and another on the frying pan, she carefully creates the main components of the casserole—waffles and scrambled eggs. She piles the waffles in a stack and turns off the burner under the frying pan. Before long the waffles, eggs, and syrupy sausages are layered in a mouthwatering concoction. Grandma turns the oven to low, places her casserole inside, and waltzes upstairs to get ready for company.

Tasty Questions

1. What are the main ingredients of the breakfast casserole?

2. List several advantages to serving a breakfast casserole rather than omelets, bacon, and sweet rolls.

3. List several disadvantages.

Write

Compose a clear and concise list of steps (like you would find on a recipe card) for making a Maple Sausage and Waffle Casserole.

Name

1. Use the context to develop a definition for **garrulous**.

> Old Simon Wheeler was a garrulous storyteller whose stories went on and on spinning tales first in one direction and then reversing to continue in another.
> —*Mark Twain*

2. Edit the sentence.

> **born samuel langhorne clemens mark twain grew up in hannibal missouri on the west bank of the mississippi river**

3. Choose the complex-compound sentence.

   a. When he was 21, Mark Twain fulfilled his dream and became a Mississippi riverboat pilot.

   b. Twain's pen name is a riverboat pilot's term for water that is just barely deep enough for safe passage: mark twain.

4. What is **colloquial language**?

5. Explain what you think Mark Twain meant when he wrote:

> *"My books are water; those of the great geniuses are wine. Everybody drinks water."*

Name

1. Divide the word into prefix, root, and suffix. Explain the meaning of each part: **conjecture**

2. Think of two explicit verbs that could replace **told** in this sentence.

> Mark Twain told humorous stories.

3. Identify the errors and correct them.

   a. The characters, a runaway slave and a white youth, personifies the injustices of a slaveholding society.

   b. Each of the characters bring a unique perspective.

4. Use the context to determine the meaning of the underlined word.

> Mark Twain's stories are set in a <u>mélange</u> of locations: the small mining town of Angel's Camp, the capitals of Europe, and a cave beside the muddy Mississippi.

5. Combine the short sentences into longer, more complex sentences. Keep the meaning clear and add transitional words as needed.

- The Civil War broke out.
- The Mississippi River was closed to commercial traffic.
- Riverboat pilots were no longer needed.
- Mark Twain ventured west to seek his fortune.

1. Match the word with the correct definition.

holy   having holes

holey   completely; fully

wholly   sacred

2. Correct the punctuation and spelling errors. Use the proofreading symbols.

through his final books were filled with the deprevity of human nature, Twain is cheifly remembered today for capturring the brash optimistic spirit of americans.

3. Write **single** or **plural** to label the subject.

a. Mark Twain's wit and humor enthralled lecture audiences.

b. Neither gold nor silver brought fame to Twain, the prospector.

4. Write the comparative and superlative adverbs for **often**.

5. Draw lines to label the dictionary entry.

- entry word   • pronunciation
- part of speech   • etymology
- usage example   • definition
- syllabication   • out-of-date usage

di•lap•i•date \de-,la-pe-dat\ vb –dated; -dating [L dilapidatus, pp. of dilapidare to squander, destroy, fr. Dis- + lapidare to pelt with stones, fr. Papid-, lapis stone] vt (1565) 1: to bring into a condition of decay or partial ruin <furniture is dilapidated by use> 2: archaic: SQUANDER ~ vi: to become dilapidated

1. Explain what Mark Twain meant.

"A habit cannot be thrown out the window, it must be coaxed down the stairs one step at a time." – *Pudd'nhead Wilson's Calendar*

2. Choose the correct literary term.

The human race has one really effective weapon, and that is laughter.

   ○ simile   ○ metaphor

   ○ personification

3. Add an apostrophe and dashes to make the meaning of this sentence clear.

Mark Twains childhood home Hannibal, Missouri was a frequent stop for steamboats arriving from St. Louis and New Orleans.

4. Correctly capitalize the following Twain titles.

- advice for little girls
- the celebrated jumping frog of calaveras county

5. Write the genre classification for each novel.

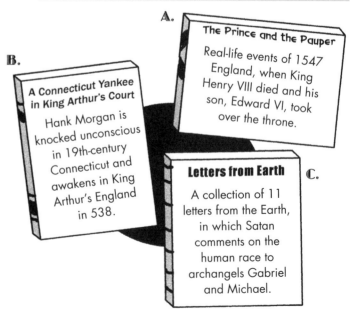

A. **The Prince and the Pauper**

Real-life events of 1547 England, when King Henry VIII died and his son, Edward VI, took over the throne.

B. **A Connecticut Yankee in King Arthur's Court**

Hank Morgan is knocked unconscious in 19th-century Connecticut and awakens in King Arthur's England in 538.

C. **Letters from Earth**

A collection of 11 letters from the Earth, in which Satan comments on the human race to archangels Gabriel and Michael.

Read

Enjoy this except from *The Celebrated Jumping Frog of Calaveras County*, the 1867 story that brought Mark Twain his first fame as a writer. Calaveras County is in Northern California. The story takes place in the early 1860s in a general store in a small mining town called Angel's Camp. Simon Wheeler, a garrulous resident of the mining camp, is describing how Jim Smiley, a local resident, trained his jumping frog.

Smiley ketched a frog one day and took him home, and said he cal'klated to edercate him; and so he never done nothing for three months but set in his back yard and learn that frog to jump. And you bet you he did learn him, too. He'd give him a little punch behind, and the next minute you'd see that frog whirling in the air like a doughnut, see im turn one summerset, or maybe a couple, if he got a good start, and come down flat-footed and all right, like a cat. He got him up so in the matter of catching flies, and kept him in practice so constant, that he'd nail a fly every time as far as he could see him. Smiley said all a frog wanted was education, and he could do most any thing—and I believe him. Why, I've seen him set Dan'l Webster down here on this floor—Dan'l Webster was the name of the frog—and sing out, "Flies, Dan'l, flies!" and quicker'n you would wink, he'd spring straight up, and snake a fly off'n the counter there, and flop down on the floor again as solid as a gob of mud, and fall to scratching the side of his head with his hind foot as indifferent as if he hadn't no idea he'd been doin' any more'n any frog might do. You never see a frog so modest and straightfor'ard as he was, for all he was so gifted. And when it come to fair and square jumping on a dead level, he could get over more ground at one straddle than any animal of his breed you ever see. Jumping on a dead level was his strong suit, you understand; and when it come to that, Smiley would ante up money on him as long as he had a red. Smiley was monstrous proud of his frog, and well he might be, for fellers that had traveled and been everywheres, all said he laid over any frog that ever they see.

From **The Celebrated Jumping Frog of Calaveras County** *by Mark Twain*

1. Identify at least two examples of colloquial language in the story. Explain which rules of grammar, spelling, or punctuation are ignored in the characters' speech.

2. What amazing things can Smiley's frog do? What personality traits does Wheeler attribute to the frog?

3. What parts of Wheeler's description do you find particularly absurd?

Write

Think of a performer who uses colloquial language and exaggeration for comic effect. How does this person's use of exaggeration compare with Wheeler's?

MONDAY WEEK 4 _____ LANGUAGE PRACTICE

Name

1. Use the context and your knowledge of root words to determine the meaning of the underlined word.

> Familiar comic–strip <u>iconography</u>—such as stars for pain, speech and thought balloons, and sawing logs for snoring—originated in Rudolph Dirk's strip, "Katzenjammer Kids".

2. Find three compound words and one additional word that are misspelled and correct them.

> In the comic strip "Pea nuts," Charlie Brown always feels <u>up set</u> after his <u>base ball</u> team <u>looses</u>.

3. Explain the usage error in the following sentence and correct it.

> **"Mutt and Jeff", was one of the most early strips to appear in color.**

4. What literary device does Garfield exemplify?

5. What made Katzenjammer Kids unique in the comic strip industry?

> • Many consider Rudolph Dirk's "Katzenjammer Kids," which appeared on December 12, 1897, in the *Journal American*, to be the first modern comic strip.

> Previously, cartoon panels had no in-panel dialogue, but in the Katzenjammer Kids dialogue was directly applied within a word balloon indicating the speaker.

> • Also, until then no strip had ever consisted of more than the single panel format of the editorial or political cartoon.

TUESDAY WEEK 4 _____ LANGUAGE PRACTICE

Name

1. Define the phrase **comic strip**.

2. Edit the following sentence.

> **in a famous comment on the ecological crisis the opossum pogo said we have met the enemy and he is us".**

3. What was Pogo's creator Walt Kelley trying to say when he wrote the comment in problem two?

4. You must write a research paper about comic strips. Narrow the broad classification to a manageable topic and write three research questions you would answer as part of your preparation for writing.

5. Edit the passage.

> **In 1924 the ~~adverchur~~ comic ~~stripe~~ was born george washington tubbs ii the ~~mane~~ character of a ~~commic~~ strip created by roy crane ~~imbarked~~ on a search for ~~baried treashure readders~~ were enthralled by the cereal cliff hangers featuring wash tubbs**

1. What is the connotation of **flagrant** in this sentence? What inferences can you make about the person who wrote the sentence?

   The comic strip "Little Orphan Annie" represents a staunch conservative viewpoint while Doonesbury represents flagrant liberalism.

2. Edit the following sentence.

   the majorety of traditionel newspaper comic strips now have some internet precense,

3. What is wrong with this sentence? Rewrite it to clarify its meaning.

   First appearing in 1919, Frank King sometimes drew innovative backgrounds for his "Gasoline Alley" strip.

4. What is the audience and the purpose of the comic in number **5**?

5. Summarize the message delivered in this comic.

1. Explain the term **caricatured**.

   Pogo's creator Walt Kelly took on Joseph McCarthy in the 1950s. He caricatured McCarthy as a bobcat named Simple J. Malarkey, a megalomaniac bent on taking over Pogo's birdwatching club and routing out all undesirables.

2. Correct the following sentence.

   Readers will often find political cartons on the editeriel page of the newpaper.

3. Rewrite this sentence so that the meaning is clear.

   In 1897 the first comic strip appeared in the *New York Journal*, called "The Yellow Kid".

4. Should comic strip characters age over time? Write a statement that explains your position.

5. Use parentheses to make the meaning clear in the following passage.

   Some comic strips are centered on human beings, but a number of strips have animals as main characters. Some of the animals are nonverbal Marmaduke, some have verbal thoughts but aren't understood by humans Garfield and Snoopy, and some can converse with humans Opus in "Bloom County" or Bucky and Satchel in "Get Fuzzy".

FRIDAY WEEK 4 _____ LANGUAGE PRACTICE

Name

Read

Nevin Katz is a science teacher in Massachusetts. He is also a cartoonist. He uses cartoons to present scientific principles to his students. Here is one of his cartoons about what cells do.

1. What is the main idea presented in this cartoon?

2. Explain how *Why Cells?* uses

• personification

• ask a question—provide the answer

• humor

• context to define words

3. Why is it easier to understand a new concept when it is presented in several different ways?

Write

Create a comic strip to explain one rule regarding comma usage. Remember that comic strips use pictures, a few words, and humor to get their point across.

          © Incentive Publications, Inc., Nashville, TN

1. Underline the simple subject in each sentence. Then circle the verb that agrees with the subject.

   a. In southwestern Texas (grow, grows) many kinds of cacti.

   b. More like the small, round cactus than one of her invaluable sewing tools, Grandmother's pincushion (stand, stands) guard at her elbow.

2. Circle the words that are synonyms for **prickly**.

   thorny   briery   troublesome

   tolerant   stinging   remorseful

3. Identify the literary device.

   The chollas grow out of the desert like enormous candelabra.

4. Edit the following sentence.

   their are about sixtie of the three thousend cactus species growwing in west texas.

5. Summarize the information in this paragraph in one or two sentences.

Like other succulents, cacti are well-adapted to life with little precipitation. For example, the leaves have evolved into spines; which, in addition to allowing less water to evaporate through transpiration than regular leaves, helps the cactus defend itself against water-seeking animals. Photosynthesis is carried out by enlarged stems, which also store water. The roots are often extensive and close to the surface of the ground, another adaptation to infrequent rains.

1. Circle things one could expect to find in a **bajada**.

   Bajadas are shallow slopes that lie at the base of rocky desert hills, where materials from weathering rocks accumulate.

   boulders   stones   rushing water

   gravel   sand   lichen and moss

2. Underline the prepositional phrase(s).

   Each aureole on the pincushion cactus has three straight central spines and a cluster of radial spines that cover the cactus.

3. Correct the spelling.

   The barrell cactus, feircely armed with heavy spins, is one of the largist cacti of the North American desserts.

4. Which words would be on the dictionary page with the guide words **rattlesnake** and **rayon**?

   raven rawhide razor rational ravine

5. Choose the complete sentence.

a. Two plants which for most of the year have photosynthetic stems instead of leaves: the ocotillo and the foothill palo verde.

b. Even so, all of these plants are specifically adapted to withstand periods of drought.

1. List three meanings of the word **stock**. Include at least one verb and one noun.

2. Identify the literary device used in the sentence.

   I hiked hither and yon that day from a hummock of limestone to a hill of gypsum, each of which harbored its own bank of cactus.

3. Add a **y** or an **e** or both to complete each word correctly.

   stingy   **troll**y   **rall**y   **air**y   **subtl**e

4. Which resource would you use to locate the range and habitat of the barrel cactus?
   a. atlas
   b. encyclopedia
   c. periodical guide
   d. thesaurus

5. Write several sentences to compare the two passages.

> In battle array, with heavy spines covering prominent ribs and a chapeau of red petals, the Ferocactus stands alone in the shadow of a canyon wall. In times past Native Americans sought him out, coveting his red petals, spines, and pulp. Today, protected from destruction by environmentalists, he waits quietly at the edge of the desert wash.

Fun With Cacti

> The barrel cactus, Ferocactus, grows along desert washes, graveled slopes, and beneath desert canyon walls. It has heavy spines covering its prominent ribs. Its red flowers always grow at the top of the plant and can be boiled in water and eaten like cabbage or mashed for a drink. Today the species enjoys a protected status in many areas.

1. Add commas to make the meaning clear.

   The edible red pulp of the organ pipe cactus can be eaten as is made into jelly, or fermented into a beverage.

2. The organ pipe cactus is found in a small area of the Sonoran Desert ranging from southwestern Arizona to western Sonora, Mexico. Would you consider this particular cactus **prevalent** or **confined**?

3. Write **who** or **whom** to complete the sentences.
   a. Who would eat candy made from a cactus?
   b. To Whom is the spiny branch most dangerous?

4. Write an interesting sentence on the flowers of the organ pipe cactus. Include these details:
   • lavender-white
   • 2 inches long
   • night-blooming in May–July
   • grow laterally near the apex of the stems

5. The name *pincushion cactus* is a metaphor. The round cactus resembles the cushion in which a seamstress sticks pins. Look at the pictures of the cacti below and give each a metaphorical name.

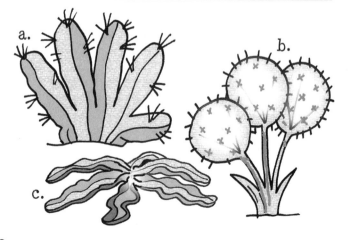

a.
b.
c.

Read O. Henry was the pseudonym of William Sydney Porter, who wrote colorful short stories with surprising and ironic twists. His best-known titles include "The Gift of the Magi" and "The Ransom of Red Chief". In his story "The Cactus," he describes a gentleman returning from the wedding of the woman he had hoped to marry.

On the table stood a singular-looking green plant in a red earthen jar. The plant was one of the species of cacti, and was provided with long, tentacular leaves that perpetually swayed . . . with a peculiar beckoning motion. . . . As he slowly unbuttoned his gloves, there passed through Trysdale's mind a swift, scarifying retrospect of the last few hours . . . in his ears was the low-pitched hum of a thousand well-bred voices, and, most insistently recurring, the drawling words of the minister irrevocably binding her to another.

Why and how had he lost her? For the thousandth time he remarshalled in his mind the events of those last few days before the tide had so suddenly turned. She had always insisted upon placing him upon a pedestal, and he had accepted her homage with royal grandeur . . . he had absorbed the oblation as a desert drinks the rain that can coax from it no promise of blossom or fruit.

He remembered the scene the night when he had asked her to come up on his pedestal with him and share his greatness. During their conversation she had said: "And Captain Carruthers tells me that you speak the Spanish language like a native. . . . Is there anything you do not know?". . . . Alas! the incense of her admiration had been so sweet and flattering. . . . Without protest, he allowed her to twine about his brow this spurious bay of Spanish scholarship. . . . He did not feel the prick of the thorn that was to pierce him later.

"I will send you my answer tomorrow," she said; and he, the indulgent, confident victor, smilingly granted the delay. The next day he waited, impatient, in his rooms for the word. At noon her groom came to the door and left the strange cactus in the red earthen jar. There was no note, no message, merely a tag upon the plant bearing a barbarous foreign or botanical name.

Ventomarme.

- -

"I say, Trysdale, what the deuce is the matter with you? You look unhappy as if you yourself had been married instead of having acted merely as an accomplice. . . . Hallo! here's an old acquaintance. Wherever did you rake up this cactus, Trysdale?"

"A present," said Trysdale, "from a friend. Know the species?"

"Very well. It's a tropical concern. See hundreds of 'em around Punta every day. Here's the name on this tag tied to it. Know any Spanish, Trysdale?"

"No," said Trysdale, with the bitter wraith of a smile—"Is it Spanish?"

"Yes. The natives imagine the leaves are reaching out and beckoning to you. They call it by this name—Ventomarme. Name means in English, 'Come and take me.'"

—from *The Cactus*
O. Henry

1. Describe the setting and main character of O. Henry's story.
2. Explain the cause of the misunderstanding between Trysdale and the lady.
3. In your opinion is the cactus an appropriate way to accept a proposal? Why or why not?

Write

Do you agree with the statement **"The presence of the cactus in Trysdale's apartment is ironic."**? Explain your position.

1. Edit the following sentence

in 1802, president jefferson offered an challange to his young assistent meriwether lewis.

2. Use the context to define **pirogue**. What is the derivation of the word?

Lewis purchased a small boat called a pirogue while he waited for the keelboat *Discovery* to be built.

3. Explain the idiom in the following sentence.

In the spring of 1804, Clark wrote in his journal, "We are fixing for a start."

4. Choose the correct word.

The paralysis _____ his limbs.
✓ ○ affected   ○ effected

5. List four objectives of Lewis and Clark's expedition to the west.

President Jefferson gave instructions to William Clark and Meriwether Lewis. Besides the main objective of the expedition, to find a route to the Pacific Ocean, the explorers were instructed to measure latitude and longitude along the way and to draw maps of the country. They were to learn about the Indian tribes along the route, studying their languages, customs, and hunting practices. If any chiefs wanted to visit Washington, Lewis and Clark were to arrange for them to come to the East. They were also to take careful notes of the climate and plant and animal life of the country they passed through.

1. Be an editor. Correct the spelling and the punctuation in this excerpt from William Clark's journal.

Ocian in view! O! The joy!

2. Underline and classify the phrase and clause in the following sentence.

After a long delay, the keelboat for the expedition was completed.

3. Lewis took vials of vermilion on the long journey. What is **vermilion**?

4. Studying Clark's journals is

a. **without merit, since the spelling and grammar are so poor**

b. **utilizing a primary source**

c. **impossible because the actual journals were lost**

5. Match the synonyms.

a. pelt
b. chore
c. reserved
d. abounding
e. aloof

1. task
2. teeming
3. hide
4. cool
5. restrained

Name

1. Define the verb **provoke**. Do you feel the connotation of the word is positive or (negative?)

2. Reorganize the sentence to clarify its meaning.

   Captain Lewis with his dog Seaman walked along the shore by his side on most days.

3. Punctuate the following sentence. Captain Lewis collected four things.

   Lewis, preserved hundreds of cuttings seeds plants and flowers.

4. Picture the explorers around their campfire. Write a simile or a metaphor to describe their appearance.

One way the men dealt with the troublesome mosquitoes was by covering themselves with grease and standing in the smoke to drive away the insects.

5. Label each statement as **fact** or **opinion**. Explain the reason for your classification.

   a. As winter progressed, the hunters had to go farther to find game.

   b. Winter was a difficult time for the members of the expedition.

   c. Many kinds of vegetation and wildlife live along the shores of the Missouri River.

   d. Today's explorers should follow the example of the Corps of Discovery.

Name

1. What is the difference between a **participle** and a **gerund**?

2. Combine the two sentences using an appositive phrase.

   Meriwether Lewis was born in 1774.

   He was the son of a Virginia planter.

3. Circle the correctly spelled words.

   (incidentally)   (preferrable)   reccommend
   (succeed)   (superceed)   unanimus

4. When would you skim an article?

   a. to evaluate the material presented

   b. to preview material before a study session

   c. to prepare to explain the information to someone else

5. Write a caption for this cartoon.

They are about to fall down a huge waterfall Oh no!

Read

Read the timeline for the Corps of Discovery's activities during 1804.

March 10
Lewis and Clark attend ceremonies in St. Louis formally transferring the Louisiana Territory to the United States.

May 14
Lewis and Clark begin journey up the Missouri River.

May 21
Corps of Discovery leaves St. Charles and embarks on journey.

July 4
The Corps holds the first Independence Day celebration west of the Mississippi river.

August 3
The Corps holds a council with the Oto and Missouri Indians.

August 20
Corps member Sergeant Charles Floyd dies of natural causes.

August 30
The Corps holds a council with the Yankton Sioux.

Early September
The Corps enters the Great Plains and sees animals unknown in the eastern United States.

September 25
The Corps has a tense encounter with the Teton Sioux.

October 24
The Corps arrives at the villages of the Mandan and Hidatsa.

November 4
Lewis and Clark hire French-Canadian fur trader Toussaint Charbonneau and his Shoshone wife, Sacagawea, to act as interpreters for the journey.

December 17
The men record the temperature at 45 degrees below zero.

December 24
The men finish building their winter quarters, Fort Mandan.

X False
O True

TRUE OR FALSE?

 1. The Corps of Discovery spent every day on the trail or river.

2. Lewis and Clark's expedition required extensive preparations

3. The members of the expeditionary force kept to themselves and simply made observations about what they observed.

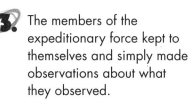 4. Lewis and Clark were self-sufficient and managed to lead their expedition without outside support.

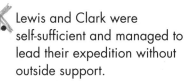 5. The exploration was quickly and easily completed in 1804.

Write

Use what you know to create a list of explicit verbs that might be used in describing Lewis and Clark's activities.

MONDAY WEEK 7 _____ LANGUAGE PRACTICE
Name

1. Some words have specific meanings when used in a mathematical context. Define each of these words in two ways: as it would be used in geometry and as you would use it in your conversation.

   • ray   • point

2. Choose the correct word.

   The bank put a _____ on his property.

   ○ line   ☑ lien

3. Diagram the sentence.

   All Math teachers give students daily homework.

4. Respond to this poetic thought.

   > He drew a circle that shut me out
   > Heretic, rebel, a thing to flout.
   > But love and I had the will to win;
   > We drew a circle that took him in.
   > Anonymous

5. Write a sentence explaining the difference between congruent figures and similar figures.

   Congruent figures have the same size and shape:
   • congruent corresponding sides
   • congruent corresponding angles

   Note: Figures can be congruent even if one of the figures is turned or flipped.

   Similar figures have the same shape, but not necessarily the same size:
   • corresponding angles are congruent
   • lengths of corresponding sides are proportional

TUESDAY WEEK 7 _____ LANGUAGE PRACTICE
Name

1. Divide the word into prefix, root, and suffix. Give the meaning of each.

   intersection

2. Add a prefix and /or a suffix to the word **symmetry** to form an adjective.

3. Edit the following sentence.

   euclids book the elements formed the basis for most of the geometry studied ever since it was written in 400 bc

4. Choose the keyword that would be **least** helpful in finding the formula for the area of a parallelogram.

   ○ **area**   ○ **quadrilateral**
   ○ **formula**   ○ **parallelogram**

5. Write a title for the figure below.

1. Write two sentences using the word **segment**. Use it as a noun in one sentence, and as a verb in the other sentence.

2. Add endings to the word **coordinate** to complete each sentence correctly.

   a. _____ are pairs of numbers that are used to determine points in a plane.

   b. _____ the football team's plays requires several coaches.

   c. The press secretary _____ the information released to the media.

3. Explain the idiom:

   a square peg in a round hole

4. Complete the sentence with the correct relative pronoun.

   The students _____ solved the problem were pleased with their accomplishment.

5. Read the notes. Write a definition for parallel lines.

- A plane is a flat surface with no thickness that extends without end in all directions on the surface.
- Two lines that lie in the same plane are either intersecting or parallel.
- Intersecting lines have exactly one point in common.
- Parallel lines have no points in common.
- Parallel segments lie in parallel lines.
- Skew lines are lines that are not parallel and do not intersect.
- Skew lines lie in different planes.
- Skew segments lie in skew lines.

1. Use the meaning of the prefix **equi-** to help choose the *equilateral triangle*.

 a   b    c

2. Rewrite this definition so it is easily understood.

   A polygon is a closed planar path composed of a finite number of sequential line segments.

3. Edit the sentence.

   any poligon reguler or ireguler has as many angels as it has sides

4. Give the past tense of each verb.

   a. intersect   b. parallel   c. admit

5. Read the bulleted information and then use it to label the two sets of figures.

   A transformation of a figure is a change in its position, shape, or size.

- a rotation is a transformation that turns a figure about a point
- a reflection is a transformation that flips a figure over a line
- a translation or slide is a transformation that moves every point of a figure the same distance and the same direction.

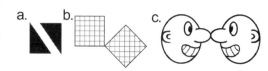

Read

Pythagoras believed that all relations could be reduced to number relations. This generalization stemmed from his observations in music, mathematics, and astronomy. Pythagoras noticed that vibrating strings produced harmonious tones when the ratios of the lengths of the strings are whole numbers, and that these ratios could be extended to other instruments. In fact, Pythagoras made remarkable contributions to the mathematical theory of music. He was a fine musician, playing the lyre.

Pythagoras studied properties of numbers that are familiar to mathematicians today, such as even, odd, and perfect numbers. Pythagoras proved the sum of the angles of a triangle is equal to two right angles, and he developed the Pythagorean theorem: In any right triangle, the sum of the squares of the lengths of the legs (a and b) is equal to the square of the length of the hypotenuse (c).

In astronomy Pythagoras taught that the earth was a sphere at the center of the universe. He also recognized that the orbit of the moon was inclined to the equator of the earth and he was one of the first to realize that Venus as an evening star was the same planet as Venus as a morning star.

1. How would you classify Pythagoras' ideas? Support your classification with facts.
   • logical   • creative   • limited   • innovative

2. True or false? Explain your answer.
   All of Pythagoras' ideas have subsequently become accepted truths.

3. In an outline of the important information in the article, what three subtopics would you choose?

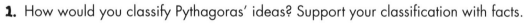

Write

A theorem is an idea accepted or proposed as a demonstrable truth. Think of an idea that you have that you believe could be a theorem about students of English. Write your theorem and list at least three facts that support it.

1. The words below have similar denotations. Tell whether each word has a positive, negative, or neutral connotation.

haughty _____   proud _____
arrogant _____   insolent _____

2. Edit the sentence.

william faulkner was borne in to a prominent southern family in missisippi

3. Change each phrase to a plural possessive form.
a. the stain made by the blueberry
b. the bite of the mosquito

4. Faulkner said, "The poet's voice need not merely be the record of man, it can be one of the props, the pillars to help him endure and prevail." Do you agree? Why or why not?

5. What literary devices does Faulkner use as he describes the house?

"Only Miss Emily's house was left, lifting its stubborn and coquettish decay above the cotton wagons and the gasoline pumps—an eyesore among eyesores."

-from the story "A Rose for Emily"

1. Write a sentence to summarize the information.
• When he was young, Faulkner was an avid reader.
• Faulkner was influeneced by his great-grandfather, who was a novelist.
• Faulkner enjoyed tales of the Civil War, folklore, French poetry, and Bible stories.

2. Circle the misspelled words.

**imperviousness   vindacate
august   obesety**

3. Edit the following sentence.

in 1926 faulkner tried his hand at fiction and published his first novel soldiers pay

4. What source would you use to find the meaning of the French expression **noblesse oblige**?

5. Match each compound word with its definition.

a. swaybacked
b. bookmark
c. ill-used
d. wrongheaded

___1. a place-keeper
___2. having a sagging spine
___3. contrary to sound judgment
___4. mistreated

1. Define the word **virulent**. Use it in a sentence.

2. Underline the main verb in the sentence.

> **Though Faulkner wrote of the conservative rural South, he <u>experimented</u> with repetition, inconsistent punctuation, and multiple points of view.**

3. What is a **flashback**?

4. Write an alliterative phrase.

5. Read the lines from the poem "Love Song." What do you think this stanza describes? How do you think the speaker felt?

> *Then shall I sit among careful cups of tea,*
> *Aware of a slight perspiring as to brow, . . .*
> *I shall sit, so patently at ease,*
> *Stiffly erect, decorous as to knees*
> *Among toy balloons of dignity on threads of talk.*

1. In accepting the Nobel Prize for Literature in 1950, William Faulkner said, "I feel that this award was not made to me as a man, but to my work. . . . So this award is only mine in trust." Explain what you think he meant.

2. Punctuate the following sentence.

> **William Faulkner, a southerner himself wrote about the conservative rural South.**

3. Would a shy newcomer be likely to demonstrate **temerity**? Explain your answer.

4. List a possible topic for a research report on William Faulkner and three questions you would ask to begin your research.

5. Combine the three short sentences to help the flow.

- **William Faulkner experimented with inconsistent punctuation.**
- **He often utilized repetition, long and puzzling sentences, and multiple points of view.**
- **William Faulkner wrote in a stream-of-consciousness style.**

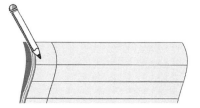

Read

Read this description from *As I Lay Dying* written by William Faulkner.

> Standing in a litter of chips, he is fitting two of the boards together. Between the shadow spaces they are yellow as gold, like soft gold, bearing on their flanks in smooth undulations the marks of the adze blade: a good carpenter, Cash is. He holds the two planks on the trestle, fitted along the edges in a quarter of the finished box. He kneels and squints along the edge of them, then he lowers them and takes up the adze. A good carpenter. Addie Bundren could not want a better one, a better box to lie in. It will give her confidence and comfort. I go on to the house, followed by the Chuck. Chuck. Chuck. of the adze.

—from *As I Lay Dying* by William Faulkner, written in 1930

1. Who is Faulkner describing?

2. What is he making?

3. What observations can you make about Faulkner's style from this excerpt?

Write

William Faulkner sometimes wrote long puzzling sentences and used punctuation that broke all of the rules. Try your hand at describing something happening in your world. Jot down your thoughts, paying careful attention to descriptive phrases and words that create "pictures" in your readers' minds. Don't worry about the rules for using end punctuation and commas. Use punctuation to indicate pauses in your thinking.

1. Rewrite each name using correct capitalization.

   a. university of arizona

   b. u. of a.

   c. k.s.u.

   d. florida state university

   e. lewis and clark university

   f. stanford university

2. Edit the sentence.

   Niether hard work nor lack of sleep deter Benjamin.

3. Circle the misspelled words.

   pasttime   **elegible**   **libary**

   separate   **occasion**   **efficient**

4. What is an adverb clause?

5. What is the main idea?

In high school, it seems like everyone has an opinion (and a bone to pick) about what it takes to get into a college. Poor test-takers think the SATs must be the most important thing. Those with lots of extracurricular activities fear that colleges will focus more on "numbers." Those who take difficult courses worry that colleges will only look at grades, and not how they were earned. In the end, the process of getting into college is usually quite fair. With a few minor exceptions, colleges are legitimately looking for the most qualified applicants they can find, and that means sifting through as much information as they have available.

—James Brody

1. Which format should be used in asking for information about a university program?

   ○ friendly letter   ○ business letter

2. Edit the sentence.

   Every period and comma were scrutinized.

3. Pasha is developing a list of adjectives to use to describe a successful student. Edit the list for her.

   eficient   **accommadating**

   disciplined   **consceintious**

   humerous   **versetile**

4. Circle the noun clause.

   Whoever reads enjoys the library.

5. Describe what you think makes a student successful.

Success is . . .

1. What is wrong with this sentence?

Javiar, as well as Simone, plan to attend Columbia University.

2. Match the meaning with the word.
Use each word correctly in a sentence.

than •   • **at that time**

then •   • **in comparison with**

3. Add correct punctuation to this quotation.

Colin Powell reported I was born in Harlem raised in the South Bronx went to public school got out of public college went into the Army and then I just stuck with it.

4. Describe a **soliloquy**.

5. Which college would be the best choice for a potential student who wants personal attention from professors in the classroom and doesn't like math? Tell why.

Massachusetts Institute of Technology
MIT is possibly the world's leading university in the areas of science and technology. While MIT students can receive a traditional liberal arts education, the school draws those with interests in such scientific fields as physics, computer science, and biotechnology.

Amherst College
Although smaller than its Ivy League counterparts, this school is no less competitive. Nestled in the hills of Western Massachusetts on a sprawling campus, Amherst is located near Emily Dickinson's home. Amherst's professors spend less time on big research projects and more time in the classroom.

1. Which closing is most appropriate for a letter accompanying a college application?

   a. Love,   c. Yours truly,

   b. Most sincerely, d. Awaiting your reply,

2. Edit the sentence.

Each of the students write an essay for their college application.

3. Correct the spelling.

Hernando read the phamflet about financal aide before filing out the questionaire.

4. Eliminate the wordiness.

In my personal opinion, it is necessary that we should not ignore the opportunity to think over each and every suggestion.

5. Classify the examples by matching them to the type of evidence they represent.

• **University freshman pay an average of $19,000 in fees.**

• **More National Merit scholars attend O.U. than any other university.**

• **College is the best time of your life.**

• **Many students protest the cost of tuition because they cannot afford to pay the fees.**

• **At some universities, out-of-state fees are waived for individuals. For example, at U.N.C., residence hall counselors from outside Colorado pay in-state tuition.**

fact

statistic

example

opinion

reason

Read

Most universities have quirky traditions that developed over the years and have been passed on from one generation of students to the next. At the University of Maryland, students rub the nose of Testudo, the diamondback terrapin, for good luck. The bronze turtle statue sits in the center of campus in front of the library, where it was mounted to a cement pedestal in the 1960s to prevent rival students from stealing it.

Other universities also claim to have statues that bring good luck. At Harvard University, you can see an aging statue of John Harvard with a very shiny foot. Students and visitors rub the statue's left shoe for good luck. Ironically, the statue is nicknamed the "Statue of Three Lies" since all three pieces of information on the inscription—John Harvard, Founder, 1638—are incorrect.

Many university traditions are linked to sports. At University of Oklahoma football games, each touchdown is succeeded by an appearance of the Sooner Schooner. The small covered wagon, pulled by two white ponies, drives onto Owen Field, makes a small loop, and heads back into a tunnel in the stadium. The Sooner Schooner got its name from the pioneers who participated in the Oklahoma Land Run in 1889. The "sooners" were the pioneers who sneaked across the line early to get the best tracts of land.

Another popular football tradition is the Gator Chomp at the University of Florida. Fans in the stadium open and close their extended arms to intimidate their opponents by simulating the chomping jaws of their mascot, the Gator.

One of the universities best known for its traditions is Texas A&M University in College Station, Texas. From Midnight Yell practice and giant bonfires to the largest military marching band, the traditions of Texas A & M date back to the university's roots in 1876. The traditions also reflect A&M's strong military ties. Every visitor to Texas A&M can experience one of the friendliest university traditions: simply stroll across campus and wait for every passing student to greet you with a "Howdy!"

1. What is a **tradition**?

2. How did the Oklahoma Sooners get their nickname?

3. Write three supporting details for the thesis: **Many university traditions are linked to sports.**

4. What do the Statue of Three Lies and the bronze statue of Testudo have in common?

Write

Describe a tradition at your school that has been handed down from one graduating class to another. Is the tradition based on superstition or cultural heritage?

1. Give the meaning of **simultaneously**.

2. Edit the sentence.

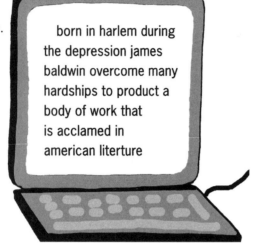

born in harlem during the depression james baldwin overcome many hardships to product a body of work that is acclamed in american literture

3. Replace the homonyms in this sentence with the correct words.

James Baldwin insisted that everyone must no his or her passed and present reality, and that one must commit oneself to act upon that understanding to.

4. Underline the adjective clause in the sentence.

Disillusioned about the prospect of social change in the United States, James Baldwin moved to Europe in 1969.

5. Choose the pair of words that best completes the analogy.

```
terrified:frightened::
____sadness:tears
____brick:hard
____starving:hungry
```

1. An essay is

a. the exploration of a topic by summarizing the opinions of other writers

b. a short, nonfiction work that explores the author's opinions and ideas on a topic

c. an anonymous traditional story passed down orally long before being written down

2. Use **loitering** in a sentence that shows you understand what the word means.

3. Edit the sentence.

james baldwins first novel go tell it on the mountain was published in 1953 and became an important portrait of life in the united states

4. What information must be included in a bibliographic entry for a novel?

5. Have you ever known someone who chose to side with a close friend or family member even though it meant breaking the rules? Explain what the rule-breaker chose to do and what happened as a result of his or her actions.

1. Choose the example of **hyperbole**.

   a. I'm so hungry I could eat a horse.

   b. bright darkness or wise fool

   c. Did you see the gymnast whirl in the air like a doughnut?

2. What is a **foil** in literature?

3. Critics say that James Baldwin exposed his readers to basic truths about the society in which they lived with uncompromising realism. What does the phrase **uncompromising realism** mean?

4. Write a sentence using each word correctly.

   • formally

   • formerly

5. In ***Nobody Knows My Name*** James Baldwin wrote:

"Yet it is only when a man is able, without bitterness or self-pity, to surrender a dream he has long cherished or a privilege he has long possessed that he is set free—for higher dreams, for greater privileges."

Do you agree or disagree? Give reasons for your opinion.

_____

_____

_____

1. Explain and correct what is wrong with the following.

   He left without saying good-bye. His anger apparent.

2. James Baldwin is said to "raise an eloquent voice in protest and social outrage against racial inequality." What does that mean?

3. Correct the misspelled words.

   absense   **accidentelly**

   acomodate   **alot**

4. The special dictionary with a collection of synonyms is called a _____.

5. Write a sentence that summarizes the following notes:

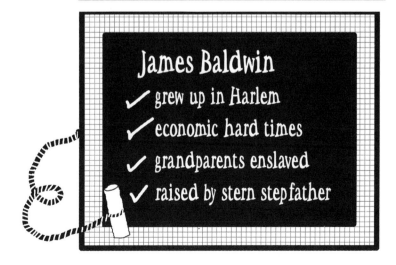

James Baldwin
✓ grew up in Harlem
✓ economic hard times
✓ grandparents enslaved
✓ raised by stern stepfather

Read

Read the passage from ***Go Tell It on the Mountain*** by James Baldwin.

The Sunday morning service began when Brother Elisha sat down at the piano and raised a song. This moment and this music had been with John, so it seemed, since he had first drawn breath. It seemed that there had never been a time when he had not known this moment of waiting while the packed church paused—the sisters in white, heads raised, the brothers in blue, heads back; the white caps of the women seeming to glow in the charged air like crowns, the kinky, gleaming heads of the men seeming to be lifted up—and the rustling and the whispering ceased, ...

1. Use the context to determine and write the meaning of the phrase "**raised a song**". What literary device does its represent?

2. What word would you use to name the mood Baldwin has created with this description?

3. Baldwin goes on to describe the singing saying,

   "They sang with all the strength that was in them, and clapped their hands for joy. There had never been a time when John had not sat watching the saints rejoice with terror in his heart, and wonder. Their singing caused him to believe in the presence of the Lord; indeed, it was no longer a question of belief, because they made that presence real."

   Explain Baldwin's use of the words—**terror** and **wonder**. How can the use of the two opposing words describe a single moment? Is there another pair of words in the paragraph that represents a similar conflict?

Write

Think about your own life. Choose a moment that has been with you since you first drew breath—a constant that you remember. Write a description of the moment. Then tell what the moment means to you.

1. Tell what is incorrect, then fix it.

The team can't change their score after the buzzer.

2. Circle the incorrectly spelled words.

eligable	**physical**	**balet**
hygeine	**versatile**	**conscientious**

3. Add endings to the word **athlete** to match each definition.

a. characteristic of an athlete—vigorous, active

b. exercises, sports, or games engaged in by athletes

c. ringworm of the feet _____ foot

4. _____ occurs when a sound, word, phrase, or line is repeated within a piece of writing.

5. Read the graph. What was the change in the record from 1865–1923?

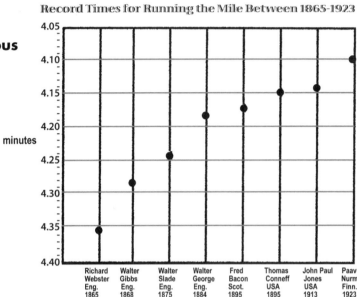

Record Times for Running the Mile Between 1865-1923

TUESDAY WEEK 11 _____ LANGUAGE PRACTICE
Name

1. Edit the sentence.

Peanut butter and jelly is a favorite among hungry skiers.

2. Complete each sentence with the correct word.

past   passed

a. John _____ Jim before the first curve.

b. The team can't change its _____ record.

3. Change both the subject and the predicate to make them **compound**.

Coaches teach players useful strategies.

4. Write an original sentence using the verbal phrase **putting pads on the floor**.

5. Write a summary of the information shown below:

Using the Dewey Decimal System

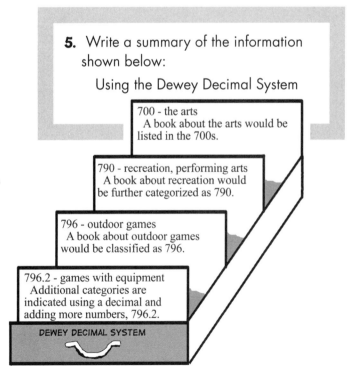

700 - the arts
A book about the arts would be listed in the 700s.

790 - recreation, performing arts
A book about recreation would be further categorized as 790.

796 - outdoor games
A book about outdoor games would be classified as 796.

796.2 - games with equipment
Additional categories are indicated using a decimal and adding more numbers, 796.2.

DEWEY DECIMAL SYSTEM

1. Write the following sentences as **inverted sentences**.

   a. Five prize trophies are there in the display case.

   b. The members of the winning team are waiting here in the gym.

2. Circle the correct verb.

Twelve months (has/have) passed since the last championship match.

3. Write an antonym for each word.

   a. contradict   b. agility

   c. determined   d. stringent

   e. benevolent   f. dehydrate

4. What literary device is used in this comparison?

Swimmers are human missiles launched underwater—well-tuned machines pitted against the clock.

5. Compare an athlete to an object in a sentence. Your words should "draw a picture" for your readers.

AN ATHLETE IS LIKE A _____ BECAUSE. . .

1. Explain why the verb is singular.

The cumulative score of the divers surprises the coach.

2. Circle the correct word.

(Who, Whom) do you think was the guest of honor?

3. Add the suffix **-able** to the word **change**.

4. What types of resources would you find when you use the *Readers' Guide to Periodical Literature*?

5. Combine each cluster of statements into one or two sentences.

   a–1 The staging area was noisy.

   –2 The staging area was cramped.

   –3 The chairs rocked back and forth as swimmers filed in and out.

   –4 It was a sea of oiled bodies and latex swim caps.

   b–1 Mark sat with seven other swimmers.

   –2 He tried to relax.

   –3 He felt tense.

   c–1 The clerk called Mark's heat.

   –2 He scrubbed his hands on his sweatshirt.

   –3 He pulled the shirt over his head.

   –4 He adjusted his goggles.

   –5 He walked toward the blocks with confidence.

Clerk of the Course

Name

Read

Read the famous poem *Casey at the Bat* by Ernest L. Thayer. It was first published on June 3, 1888, in the *San Francisco Examiner*. Actor and speaker De Wolf Hopper recited the poem during a performance at the Wallack Theater before an audience of baseball players and it was an instant success.

The outlook wasn't brilliant for the Mudville nine that day;
The score stood four to two, with but one inning more to play,
And then when Cooney died at first, and Barrows did the same,
A pall-like silence fell upon the patrons of the game.

A straggling few got up to go in deep despair. The rest
Clung to that hope which springs eternal in the human breast;
They thought, "If only Casey could but get a whack at that—
We'd put up even money now, with Casey at the bat."

But Flynn preceded Casey, as did also Jimmy Blake,
And the former was a hoodoo, while the latter was a cake;
So upon that stricken multitude grim melancholy sat;
For there seemed but little chance of Casey getting to the bat.

But Flynn let drive a single, to the wonderment of all,
And Blake, the much despised, tore the cover off the ball;
And when the dust had lifted, and men saw what had occurred,
There was Jimmy safe at second and Flynn a-hugging third.

Then from five thousand throats and more there rose a lusty yell;
It rumbled through the valley, it rattled in the dell;
It pounded on the mountain and recoiled upon the flat,
For Casey, mighty Casey, was advancing to the bat.

There was ease in Casey's manner as he stepped into his place;
There was pride in Casey's bearing and a smile lit Casey's face.
And when, responding to the cheers, he lightly doffed his hat,
No stranger in the crowd could doubt 'twas Casey at the bat.

Ten thousand eyes were on him as he rubbed his hands with dirt.
Five thousand tongues applauded when he wiped them on his shirt.
Then while the writhing pitcher ground the ball into his hip,
Defiance flashed in Casey's eye, a sneer curled Casey's lip.

And now the leather-covered sphere came hurtling through the air,
And Casey stood a-watching it in haughty grandeur there.
Close by the sturdy batsman the ball unheeded sped—
"That ain't my style," said Casey. "Strike one!" the umpire said.

From the benches, black with people, there went up a muffled roar,
Like the beating of the storm-waves on a stern and distant shore;
"Kill him! Kill the umpire!" shouted someone on the stand;
And it's likely they'd have killed him had not Casey raised his hand.

With a smile of Christian charity great Casey's visage shone;
He stilled the rising tumult; he bade the game go on;
He signaled to the pitcher, and once more the dun sphere flew;
But Casey still ignored it, and the umpire said, "Strike two!"

"Fraud!" cried the maddened thousands, and echo answered, "Fraud!"
But one scornful look from Casey and the audience was awed.
They saw his face grow stern and cold, they saw his muscles strain,
And they knew that Casey wouldn't let that ball go by again.

The sneer has fled from Casey's lip, the teeth are clenched in hate;
He pounds with cruel violence his bat upon the plate.
And now the pitcher holds the ball, and now he lets it go,
And now the air is shattered by the force of Casey's blow.

Oh, somewhere in this favored land the sun is shining bright,
The band is playing somewhere, and somewhere hearts are light,
And somewhere men are laughing, and little children shout;
But there is no joy in Mudville—mighty Casey has struck out.

1. Use the context of the poem to define each of these words.

   • **bade**   • **doffed**   • **wonderment**
   • **awed**   • **favored**   • **maddened**

2. How can a tongue applaud?

3. What does it mean to **hug third**?

4. When Blake **tore the cover off the ball** what did he do?

Write

Which literary device was most important to Thayer's poem? Select one and write a paragraph that presents the reasoning for your selection.

• **repetition**   • **characterization**
• **humor**   • **surprise ending**

1. Edit the sentence.

while in chicago I hope to see the drowsy chaperone hairspray and the producers

2. What is the subject of the sentence?

Please arrive at least 30 minutes before curtain time.

3. List four attributes of a play.

4. Fat Joe, the proprietor of a bar in London, opens Eugene O'Neill's play *The Long Voyage Home.* Use these lines to determine the type of bar.

JOE—(yawning) Blimey if bizness ain't 'arf slow tonight. I donnow wot's 'appened. The place is like a bleedin' tomb. Where's all the sailor men, I'd like to know?

○ hopping joint   ○ deserted dive

5. Define the following theater terms:

ONSTAGE _____

apron _____

wings _____

house _____

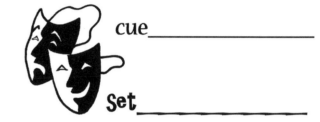

cue _____

set _____

1. John Caird and Trevor Nunn adapted Victor Hugo's novel *Les Miserables* for the theater. What does this mean?

2. Edit the sentence.

Rent a study of young hungry artists in new york citys east village is a modern interpretation of the opera la boheme.

3. Correct these misspelled words.

directer   maneger   operater

4. Do you agree or disagree? Support your opinion.

5. Describe these citations.
- **parenthetical documentation**
- **footnotes**
- **endnotes**

In a drama, dialogue is more important than action in helping the reader learn about the characters.

1. When you read or see a play, the sequence of plot events builds to a point at which you feel the greatest emotional intensity or suspense. This point is called the _____.

2. What is a **protagonist**?

3. Edit the sentence.

   the cruicble dramatizes the story of a historical incident in seventeenth-century salem massachusetts in which accusations made by young women sets off a witch hunt.

4. Choose the word that best completes the analogy.

   clear : puzzle :: conciliatory : _____

   ○ gesture   ○ threat   ○ success

5. Read the ticket. Record the following information.
   • day of performance
   • time of performance
   • cost of ticket
   • venue
   • location of seat

1. Tell what may be wrong and write three ways to solve the problem.

   A **playwright** must make careful word choices in **his** work.

2. A playwright writes **stage directions**. Explain what that entails.

3. What is a **monologue**?

4. Number the list of playwrights in alphabetical order. (Use last names.)

   ___ Arthur Miller

   ___ William Shakespeare

   ___ Albert Camus

   ___ Neil Simon

   ___ Moliere

   ___ Aeschylus

5. Mark the seat *Orchestra, K-16* on the diagram of the theater.

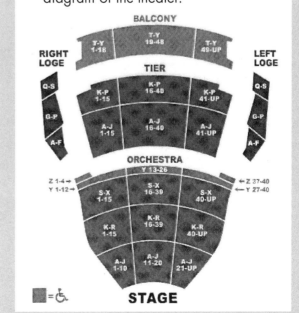

Theater & Arts

Thursday, Dec. 5

Read

The Phantom of the Opera

In the role of Christine, Rosie Herman's effortless soprano voice and agile feet overshadowed John Robertson's gravelly baritone and sloppy depiction of the choreography as the Phantom. The swooping chandelier was impressive, as were the costumes in the chorus number "Masquerade," though a few more hours in the studio might have helped with the dancers' synchronization. By the end of the second act, the audience's mood was gloomier than the Phantom's dungeon. Herman was the only bright light in an otherwise dismal performance.

Oklahoma

Grab your lasso, pull on that cowboy hat, and hustle down to the Country Theater to see this fantastic revival of a Roger and Hammerstein classic. From the opening number "Oh, What a Beautiful Morning," to the rousing favorite "Surrey With the Fringe on Top," Oklahoma feels like a boot-scootin' hoe down. Just like the wind sweeping down the plains, this production will blow you away.

Lion King

The magnificent costumes and enchanting music of "The Lion King" transported the breathless audience from the Civic Theater to the African Sahara for an unforgettable evening. The puppeteers maneuvered the complex animal costumes with remarkable agility and realism, blending into the subtle backdrops depicting the dry, arid landscape. Out of these beautiful surroundings, the pure voices of classically trained vocalists soared above the stage, penetrating the hearts and souls of all present. "The Lion King" was truly an out-of-this-world experience and a night to remember.

Grease

The Corvette Theater Company pulls off a mediocre, but entertaining, production of this bobby-sock classic. Lily Moon steals the show as a spunky and innocent Sandy who blossoms from a prim bookworm into a confident co-ed. Danny, portrayed by Scott Carpenter, and his gang of buddies, the T-Birds, warble through their musical numbers but keep the audience laughing with their slapstick antics. Despite a few missed notes and technical hitches, everyone left the theater smiling after an energetic curtain call.

1. Which Broadway show was the reviewer's favorite? Give reasons for your opinion.
2. Using the cues from the reviews, think of one classification that would fit all the shows.
3. List three adjectives for each of the following actors: Rosie Herman, John Robertson, Lily Moon, Scott Carpenter. Then rate their performances as excellent, good, or poor.
4. What writing mode is a Broadway review?
5. Which musical would you rather see and why?

Write

Write two reviews of the same event. Use tone and word choice to make one review positive and one review negative.

1. Underline the complete predicate.

Species that receive protection under the ESA are classified into two categories, "Endangered" or "Threatened," depending on their status and how severely their survival is threatened.

2. Choose the correct pronoun.

_____ makes the final decision about the classification of endangered animals?

○ Who   ○ Whom

3. Add punctuation to this quotation.

Ever since before the beginning of recorded history, Jan Goble suggests man has played a decisive role in the quality of his environment and the loss of life in it.

4. Circle the correctly spelled words.

reptile   fatel   shrivle   frugal

5. What is the main idea?

An outbreak of Ebola virus in the northwestern Republic of Congo has killed 5,000 gorillas, helping to push the threatened species closer to extinction. The Lossi outbreak killed about as many gorillas as survive in the entire eastern gorilla species. When losses from commercial hunting are added to the statistics, scientists predict a rapid ecological extinction.

1. What is the meaning of the prefix **para-**?

2. Write a strong thesis statement for a persuasive paragraph on the importance of protecting endangered animals.

3. Edit the following sentence.

the shady persuit of endangered bird eggs made International headlines when Colin Watson widely considered britain's most notoriaus ilegal egg collecter died after falling from a 12-meter tree while hunting a rare egg.

4. Document the source using appropriate format.

The Third Chimpanzee: The Evolution and Future of the Human Animal

by Jared Diamond

Harper Perennial, 1992, Chicago, IL

5. Define a secondary consumer using the labeled diagram.

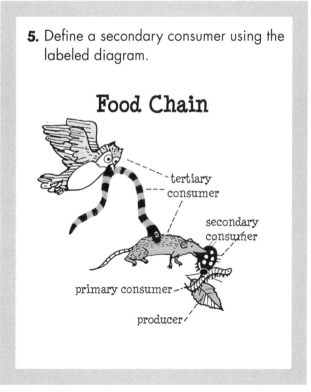

Food Chain

tertiary consumer

secondary consumer

primary consumer

producer

WEDNESDAY WEEK 13 _____ LANGUAGE PRACTICE
Name

1. Write two synonyms for **endangered**.

2. Change each phrase to a plural possessive.
   one rhino's horn
   the beetle's shell
   a t-rex's roar

3. Choose the correct word.

   One of the _____ of man's progress is a diminished natural habitat for many animals.

   ○ affects   ○ effects

4. Order the four events in a logical sequence.
   __ Native Americans hunted buffalo.
   __ Fur traders supplied manufacturers with buffalo skins.
   __ Enormous herds of buffalo roamed the plains.
   __ Wealthy Easterners enjoyed the warmth of stylish buffalo robes.

5. Analyze the rhyme pattern in this stanza from Edgar Allen Poe's "The Raven".

   Once upon a midnight dreary, while I pondered, weak and weary,

   Over many a quaint and curious volume of forgotten lore,

   While I nodded, nearly napping, suddenly there came a tapping,

   As of someone gently rapping, rapping at my chamber door.

   "'Tis some visitor," I muttered, "tapping at my chamber door—
   Only this, and nothing more."

THURSDAY WEEK 13 _____ LANGUAGE PRACTICE
Name

1. Correct the sentence.

   Each of the animals have specific requirements for survival.

2. In *Webster's Collegiate Dictionary* the word **endangered** has the date 1964 in parentheses after the entry. What does this date mean?

3. Explain the difference between **incredible** and **incredulous**.

4. Imagine that you must write a research report on some aspect of endangered animals. Choose an appropriate topic and identify three research questions you would use to begin your research.

5. Classify the following statements as fact or opinion.

   a. All development should be restricted if it threatens the habitat of an endangered species.

   B. ACRES OF RAINFOREST ARE BEING DESTROYED EVERY DAY.

   BE GREEN!

   c. The Endangered Species Act (ESA) was passed in 1973 in order to protect those plant and animal species at risk of becoming extinct.

   SAVE THE ENVIRONMENT

Read

I see her every night, her graceful lines and sleek orange and black stripes bleeding into the shadowy darkness. She is a portentous predator who moves silently and can appear and disappear in the blink of an eye. I've watched her grow from a furry cub to a lean, independent warrior, just as I watched generations before her.

But there is change in the air, and I am worried. The landscape, once lush and abundant with wildlife, has been shrinking. Over the centuries, the humans have extended their villages and towns into towering, chaotic cities. As I make my nightly rotation around the earth, I see the electric lights multiply. Every night a few more appear.

They are moving closer to her, too. She can sense it; I see her ears back and her eyes nervously searching for signs of the human intruders. Her nightly forays to find food are longer, and, often, she is still hungry at dawn. The noise and hunters have driven the animals farther into the jungle. It will be difficult for her to find a mate, to have cubs of her own.

I see the lights making their way closer to her domain from all sides. I only hope that at some point the humans will stop, that they will decide their cities are large enough. And I hope that day comes soon, because I cannot imagine my passing nightly without glimpsing her magnificence.

1. Who is the observer in this description?

2. How does the observer feel about the animal?

3. Does the observer approve of the changes noted? How can you tell? Give specific examples to support your opinion.

4. Define the following words: portentous, abundant, forays, domain.

Write

Choose an endangered animal. Write a description of the animal from the viewpoint of a partisan observer. Convey the observer's viewpoint without actually stating his or her position.

1. Read the journal entry in **5**. List three sets of antonyms found in the paragraph.

2. Edit the following sentence.

in traditional balinese mythology batara kala the god of the underworld and the creator of the light and the earth

3. Classify the sentence.

Child of All Nations is the second volume in the Bura Quartet written by Pramoedya Ananta Toer.

○ simple

○ compound

○ complex

4. Define **annihilate**.

5. Summarize the thought in Minke's Journal.

Whether light or shadow, nothing can escape being pushed along by Batara Kala. No one can return to his starting point. Maybe this mighty god is the one whom the Dutch call the Teeth of Time. He makes the sharp blunt, and the blunt sharp; the small are made big and the big made small. All are pushed on toward the horizon, while it recedes eternally beyond our reach, pushed on to annihilation. And it is that annihilation that in turn brings rebirth.

from *Child of All Nations*
written by Pramoedya Ananta Toer
translated by Max Lane

1. Which reference would be most helpful in determining the current exchange rate for the dollar in Indonesia? Why?

atlas   almanac

Internet encyclopedia

2. Circle the synonyms for **native**.

indigenous   **simple**

inborn   **natural**

3. Correct the spelling.

pupeter _____

paradice _____

humedity _____

4. When is it acceptable to use a dash in a sentence?

5. Paraphrase headlines to predict what you think the article is about.

a. Sumatra Sentinel   April, 2005
Tsunami-Ravaged Aceh Savors Gift of Peace

b. Bali Bulletin_____December, 2006
Court Jails Embassy Bomber

c. Kalimantan Clarion_____February, 2007
Asian Leaders Call for Tougher Measure to Combat Air Pollution

1. Former Indonesian president Suharto was sometimes referred to as a puppet master. What literary device is used in the statement?

2. Circle the linking verb.

I am studying the fine art of puppetry with an amazing puppet master who makes his own puppets.

3. What is a Tok Dalang?

The task of the Tok Dalang requires immense skill and endurance, for not only does he control the movements of the puppets, he also has to provide each one with a distinguishable voice, and at times, to sing, all while "conducting" the accompanying traditional music ensemble by tapping a rattle (known as the kechrek) with his feet.

4. What is the plural of **Hindu**?

Library Journal _____

5. What does the literary reviewer mean?

The imperialistic injustices of the 19th century have become the firmly institutionalized injustices of the 20th century in many countries, as evidenced by the fact that Pramoedya wrote this novel while imprisoned in Indonesia because he was considered a subversive writer.

–Brian Geary, Library Journal

1. What key words would you use to look up information about traditional Indonesian shadow puppets?

2. Use the context to define **Wayang kulit**.

Perforated leather puppets with movable, jointed arms, Wayang kulit, are popular in Indonesia.

3. True or false?

Unlike possessive nouns, possessive pronouns never have apostrophes.

4. Does the author like Wayang Kulit? Support your opinion.

A spellbinding medium for storytelling, the Wayang Kulit is a traditional theatre form that brings together the playfulness of a puppet show, and the elusive quality and charming simplicity of a shadow play.

5. Edit the notecard.

WAYANG PUPPETRY

● a traditional indonesian puppet play last about seven hours.

● gongs drums and xylophones provides back ground music

● beautiful leather puppets are neatly arrange their body-sticks firmly planted in banana stems

● good characters on the right hand side the bad on the left

● the play begins with a knock on the puppet chest

Read

Indonesia

In Jakarta and throughout Indonesia, modern technology and ancient traditions blend together. High-rise skyscrapers stand beside historic mosques; high-speed jets land on runways next to rice fields that are cultivated by farmers using the same methods as their ancestors. The modern-day nation of Indonesia is only 60 years old, but the variety of religious and cultural influences and the amazing architectural ruins that are scattered across the islands show the centuries of history that have shaped this remarkable place. From the ninth century Buddhist temple, Borobudur, to the Hindu island of Bali, the largest Muslim nation in the world truly takes to heart its national motto, "Unity in Diversity."

Indonesia's diversity also extends to its ecology. Komodo dragons, orangutans, rhinos, and seahorses are just a few of the animals that reside in Indonesia's rain forests, beaches, coral reefs, swamps, and mangroves. Indonesia may seem like a tropical paradise, but the same geographic and natural forces that make it beautiful also make it unpredictable. Located near three major tectonic plates and dotted with more than 60 volcanoes, the islands of Indonesia face frequent natural disasters such as earthquakes, volcanic eruptions, and tsunamis. One recent devastating event was a tsunami caused by an earthquake in the Indian Ocean. The giant wave struck the island of Sumatra on December 26, 2004. It killed more than 150,000 people in Indonesia and thousands more around the region. The area struck by the tsunami is rebuilding, but it was a major blow to the nation of Indonesia and will go down as one of the saddest chapters in Indonesia's long and fascinating history.

The nation of Indonesia covers a vast expanse of the Pacific Ocean astride and south of the Equator. It consists of more than 17,000 islands, 6,000 of which are uninhabited. With more than 220 million citizens, Indonesia is the world's fourth most populous nation. The national language of Indonesia is Bahasa Indonesia. Most Indonesians also speak at least one of the nation's 700 local languages or dialects in addition to Bahasa Indonesia and English. The capitol city of Jakarta is a bustling metropolitan area with more than eight million residents.

1. List four facts presented in the sidebar.

2. Choose one word that could be the theme of the article excerpt. Explain why you chose that word.

3. Write a sentence that compares the natural disasters common to Indonesia with natural disasters that may occur in the area where you live.

4. Explain the meaning of the phrase **takes to heart**.

Write

Using the word you chose as the theme of the excerpt for your topic, outline the relevant information.

1. Is the verb transitive or intransitive?

A fierce storm blew across the waves.

2. Choose the answer that is the best beginning for the sentence. It should be clear and precise.

_____ **is now a busy teen meeting place.**

○ The skate park, once about to close due to lack of funds,. . .

○ The skate park was once about to close due to lack of funds, it . . .

○ The skate park that once having been about to close due to lack of funds . . .

3. List three precise words that describe how a skydiver moves.

4. What does the word **agape** mean?

Matt's mouth was agape and his face was white as he watched the bungee-jumper.

5. Correct the spelling on the signs.

Climb Mt. Heart Attack

a. PREPOSTERUS!

b. Iresistable!

c. UNTHINKIBLE!

d. Absolutly Not!

1. Locate the incorrect word. Cross it out and replace it with a correctly spelled word.

The skier performed three twists and a flip in the air. That's inedible!

2. Write a smashing opening sentence for a soccer newsletter that will command the readers' rapt attention.

3. Circle the best source if you're curious about the world record for the longest luge ride.

encyclopedia index

almanac

The Guinness Book of World Records

biographical dictionary

4. What would you do with a **bialy**?

○ plant it   ○ cook it

○ sing to it   ○ sign it

5. Match the antonyms.

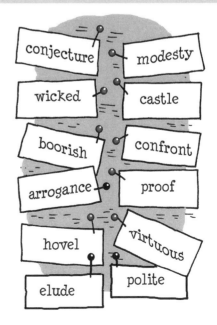

conjecture

modesty

wicked

castle

boorish

confront

arrogance

proof

hovel

virtuous

elude

polite

1. Complete the word by adding the root that has the meaning given.

   sus _____ **(hang)**

2. Clarify the meaning by rewriting the sentence.

   The fans booed the football players in the stands.

3. Choose the correct word.

   Did you and (he, him) survive the wild raft ride?

4. Think of verbs with the given meanings to complete the sentence.

   The athletes _____ out onto the field.

   _____ (make them enthusiastic)

   _____ (make them angry)

5. Number the sentences in chronological order.

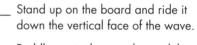

HOW TO SURF

___ Stand up on the board and ride it down the vertical face of the wave.

___ Paddle out to the area beyond the breaking waves.

___ Start by kneeling or lying on the surfboard.

___ Wait for the right wave.

___ If you time it right, the wave will pick up your surfboard and carry it along.

___ When you see one coming, turn and paddle furiously to shore.

1. Are all skateboarders **obstreperous**? Why or why not?

2. Circle the subject. Underline the direct object.

   Tumbling down the hill is not what I wanted to do today.

3. Capitalize words correctly in the lead sentence for this news article.

   in the marathon leg of the 1989 ironman triathlon in hawaii, jim maclaren, a 27-year-old professional triathlete and a former linebacker for yale, fell in step with 41-year-old ken mitchell, who played the same position for the atlanta falcons.

4. Should you run a marathon if you're **enervated**? Why or why not?

5. On what pages will you find info about cardiovascular exercise?

   education, brain function, 87-90

   elastin, 253

   elliptical machine, 133

   enzymes, 185, 205

   exercise, 5, 8, 11, 27, 34, 40, 52, 53, 55, 56, 160, 334

      for bone-building , 123-39

      cardiovascular, 27, 49-50, 51, 151

      controlling blood pressure, 310

      heart rate elevation and, 133

      obesity as obstacle to, 125

      and osteoporosis prevention, 109

Read

Zipping, snapping, jacket-strapping,
Unloading, inflating, both hands heaving, splashing, boarding, concentrating,
Flowing, gurgling, soft, meandering, reaching, pulling, synchronizing, laughing, chatting,
Tummies fluttering,
Towering, threatening, valley narrowing,
Rushing, foaming, blue-green swirling, straining,
Shouting, motivating, swooping, spinning, jaw-bone rattling,
Thrilling, chilling, heartbeat quickening,
Sputtering,
Yawing, gently dipping,
Leveling, drifting, pacifying,
Dripping, drooping, reminiscing, smiling, drying —satisfied!

---

1. What sport might the author of the poem be describing?

2. The majority of the words in the poem are gerunds. What is a gerund?

3. Complete the analogy.
   jaw-bone rattling : scared :: _____ : overjoyed

4. Describe the pace of the poem. It begins quickly. Then what happens?

5. Write a synonym for each verb.
   meander   narrow   pacify   satisfy

Write

A few well-chosen words can create a mood and describe an experience Write a poem using only a few words. Traditional sentence structure is not necessary. You have poetic license to create your own kinds of sentences.

1. Use the verbal phrase in an original sentence.

scurrying onto the train

2. Identify the literary device used.

The tunnel swallowed the train as it rushed to take its riders home.

3. Explain the underlined phrase.

Expanding transportation options for seniors will allow older citizens to "age in place" within their own neighborhoods with easy access to essential, everyday destinations.

4. Edit the sentence.

Congeschun and trafic problems are no longer confined to only the most largest of metropoliton areas.

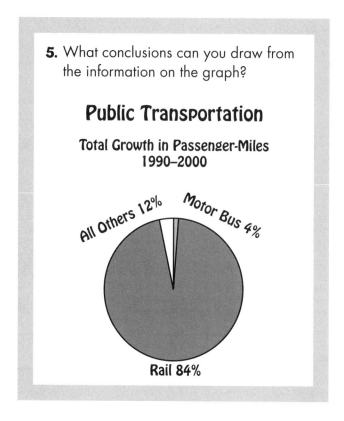

5. What conclusions can you draw from the information on the graph?

Public Transportation

Total Growth in Passenger-Miles 1990–2000

All Others 12%
Motor Bus 4%
Rail 84%

1. Brainstorm possible research topics for a report on public transportation. List at least three.

2. What's wrong with the following sentence?

Sophie and Martin are riding the ferry for the first time, they are very excited.

3. Edit the quotation for punctuation.

It seems imperative reports Richard J. Jackson M.D. that new transportation options be developed and implemented in order to help alleviate the public health problems related to worsening air quality

4. Ridership on one Express line in Atlanta, GA, increased 121% for November from 2004 to 2005. What might have caused the increase?

5. Summarize the information on the notecard.

Harris Interactive National Survey (adults aged 65 and older)

● 4 out of 5 seniors say public transportation is better than driving alone, especially at night.

● 83% of those over 65 believe public transportation gives easy access to life's needs.

● $\frac{2}{3}$ of seniors believe communities need more public transportation.

1. What is a **ballad**?

2. Rewrite to change the tense of the sentence from past to present perfect. Add an adverb or adverb phrase to show that the action began in the past and continues into the present.

My parents parked in the commuter lot.

3. Circle the correctly spelled words.

commutter	transpertation
intersection	benefits

4. Does your experience support this statement? Write a sentence about traffic congestion.

A recent survey reported: Each person traveling in peak periods wastes, on average, 62 hours a year—nearly eight full working days—in traffic congestion delays.

5. Analyze the poster. Explain the idiom and the metaphor. Explain whether you think the slogan is an effective tool for persuading people to use public transportation.

GET ON BOARD

No. 10

Springfield Transit Lines

Public Transportation Is the Key To Energy Independence

1. Write each noun as a plural.

bus   ferry   trolley   taxi

2. Circle the word that is correct.

Neither of the buses (arrives or arrive) on time.

3. Analyze the columnist's word choice. Explain why you think it was effective or ineffective.

Providing fast, affordable, reliable public transportation is essential in blunting the effects of crippling congestion, and providing sustained relief.

4. Imagine a man who didn't have enough money to pay the fare. Then explain the premise behind the famous refrain.

He may ride forever 'neath the streets of Boston. He's the man who never returned

5. What is the main idea of this introductory paragraph?

Researchers combed through results from the 2001 National Household Travel Survey and examined walking times for 3,312 transit users, finding that their average walking time was nearly 25 minutes on days they used public transit, according to a study published in the November issue of the *American Journal of Preventive Medicine*. Some of these transit users may be getting the 30-plus minutes of daily moderate-to-vigorous physical activity recommended by the U.S. Surgeon General.

Read:

Transportation System Guidelines

Thank you for using the Springfield Transport System. Please read the following guidelines for your safety and convenience. Follow the signs to the proper boarding area. Check electronic bulletin boards for arrivals and departures.

Transit Rules:

1. Passengers aged 3 and over must purchase tickets.
2. Please allow the current passengers to disembark before boarding the transit.
3. Pets are not allowed.
4. Open containers of food or beverage are not permitted.
5. Roller skates, rollerblades, skateboards, and bicycles are not allowed.
6. Wait behind the yellow lines.
7. Priority seating is reserved for the elderly and disabled.

Prices:

Subway	Tram
Adult: $1.50 each stop	$2.00 one way $3.00 round trip
Senior: $1.25 each stop	$1.50 one way $2.00 round trip
Child: (3-17) $1.00 each stop	$1.50 one way $2.50 round trip

Children under 3: free

Weekly Subway Passes:
Adult: $20.00; Child: $15.00; Senior: $17.50

Regular Stops: Subway (S) Tram (T)

Main Street (S)	Porter Zoo (T)
Lincoln Park (S)	Harrington (T)
First Street (S)	Warner Hill (T)
Midtown (S) (T)	Central Park (T)
Green Ave. (S)	
Old Town (S) (T)	
West End (S)	
Claremont (S)	
Valley View (S)	
Washington Square (S) (T)	

1. How many stops would you pass by if you made a subway trip from Lincoln Park to Valley View? a tram trip from Midtown to Washington Square?

2. How are ticket prices for the tram determined?

3. How much would it cost for a family of five (two adults, three school-age children) to take the subway from Washington Square to West End twice a day for a week? Would it be more economical to purchase a weekly pass or buy individual tickets?

4. What suggestions do you have for the committee that is revising the transportation guidelines for Springfield?

Write

Take a position on the statement. Write a persuasive argument for your position. Remember to state your position clearly and support it with examples or facts.

Public transportation has a positive impact on quality of life.

1. Circle the correctly spelled words.

discepline	**misspell**
genious	**libary**
receipt	**versatle**

2. Add proper punctuation.

His mother said Quit talking foolishness!

3. Choose the correct words.

a. **The mayor's policies have (affected, effected) every city agency.**

b. **For the most part, the (affect, effect) on the agencies has been positive.**

4. What is **colloquial language**?

5. A euphemism is an agreeable or neutral word or phrase used in place of another word or phrase that is considered harsh, insensitive, or offensive.

Instead of saying someone died:

Who would have thought that the old guy would cash in his chips so soon?

or

He's pushing up daisies now.

Draw a line from each word on the left to its equivalent euphemism on the right.

- *spying*   *strategic withdrawal*
- *retreat*   *terminate*
- *fire*   *intelligence gathering*

---

1. Choose the correct word.

The opportunity (passed, past) him by before he recognized it.

2. Write an **interrogative sentence**.

3. Does the following information require documentation in a research paper?

The 1893 Columbian Exposition commemorated the 400th anniversary of Columbus's historic voyage.

4. Write two details to support this statement.

The English language has a deceptive air of simplicity.

5. An English clergyman named William Spooner had the habit of unintentionally transposing sounds from one word to another as he spoke. These humorous slips of the tongue came to be known as **spoonerisms**.

A weather forecaster's spoonerism:

Rain and slow, followed by sneet.

Unscramble these spoonerisms:

a well-boiled icicle

a blushing crow

An usher's spoonerism:

Let me sew you another sheet.

1. Carl Sandburg once said, "Slang is a language that rolls up its sleeves, spits on its hands and goes to work." Explain the metaphor; tell whether you agree, and why or why not.

2. Find the word that is misspelled. Cite the rule that applies to the spelling of the words.

truly   arguement   sincerely

3. What is **abstract language**?

4. Give the past form and the past participle for each verb.

speak

write

vorpol
uffish
tugley wood

5. Read the stanzas from Lewis Carroll's famous poem "Jabberwocky". Use the context to decipher the story and retell what happened.

He took his vorpal sword in hand:
Long time the manxome foe he sought —
So rested he by the Tumtum tree,
And stood awhile in thought.
And, as in uffish thought he stood,
The Jabberwock, with eyes of flame,
Came whiffling through the tulgey wood,
And burbled as it came!
One, two! One, two!
And through and through
The vorpal blade went snicker-snack!
He left it dead, and with its head
He went galumphing back.

1. Define and compare these three types of research papers: a **summary paper**, an **evaluative paper**, and an **original paper**.

2. Make up a new compound word. Tell what it means and use it in a sentence.

3. Write the plural of each word.

series
blackberry
attorney general

4. Classify the clause *who are afraid of heights*.

People who are afraid of heights, acrophobics, do not like to look down from balconies or terraces.

5. Read the note. Then match the eponyms with the correct words.

William Penn, George W. G. Ferris, and Louis Pasteur are all eponyms. An eponym is a person whose name is the source for the name of someone or something. The Ferris wheel was named for George W. G. Ferris; Louis Pasteur gave his name to his discovery, the process of sterilizing milk; and a state was named after William Penn.

a temperature scale   Adolphe Sax

unit of electricity   Gabriel Fahrenheit

a wind instrument   James Watt

Read

"Over here, honey," Dolly beckoned toward Adam from the back corner of the garden. His shoes made sucking sounds in the muddy ground as he made his way across the mossy soil. "It's mighty wet, I know," said Dolly. "It was raining cats and dogs last night." She handed Adam a worn wicker basket and motioned toward the flowering tomato vines.

"You sure do have a green thumb, Dolly," he said, gazing at the endless rows of blossoming fruits and vegetables.

Dolly smiled. "It's that special fertilizer that cost me an arm and a leg. And all of that awful rain."

"Yeah," sighed Adam, "I guess every cloud has a silver lining." He pointed to the budding watermelon plant near the fence. "Dolly, we're going to have some delicious melon for the Independence Day Fair. You've got a blue ribbon winner there."

Dolly shook her head. "Now, now, Adam, we shouldn't count our chickens before they hatch. It's too early yet. I'll be on pins and needles until I cut a ripe melon off the vine."

"Don't worry, Dolly," reassured Adam. "Those other melons are a dime a dozen, but yours are the cat's meow!"

Dolly blushed and turned to head back to the house. "Gather up those baskets and come help me roll out the dough."

Adam grabbed a basket under each arm and started trudging back across the moist ground. "Dolly, I don't mind picking and hauling, but the day I bake a pie is the day pigs fly!"

1. List six idioms from the story and give their meaning. (Choose from the eleven included.)

2. The author's use of particular idioms reflects a variation of language or dialect. What setting do they suggest?

3. Analyze what the dialogue revealed about the two characters. Record what you know in the organizer below.

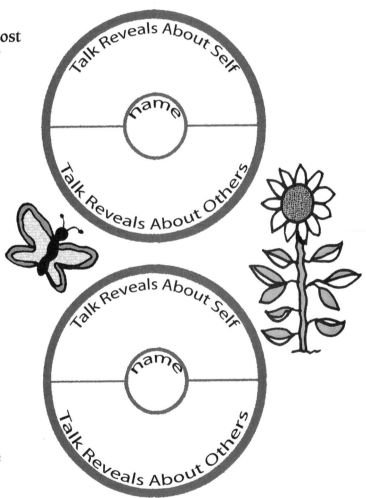

Write

Use the information you recorded to write a description of Dolly.

1. Edit the sentences.

during his lifetime robert frost recieved more awards that any other twentieth-century poet including four pulizer prizes for poetry and a congressional medal.

2. Choose the correctly spelled word to complete the sentence.

Robert Frost _____ real life experiences to academic learning.

○ prefered   ○ preferred

3. Define the underlined word.

Some critics consider Frost's treatment of subjects <u>superficial</u>.

4. Robert Frost encouraged his students at Amherst to bring the sound of the human voice to their writing. What do you think he meant?

5. Read the poem.
What is the rhyme pattern?

FIRE AND ICE

Some say the world will end in fire;
Some say in ice.
From what I've tasted of desire
I hold with those who favor fire.
But if it had to perish twice,
I think I know enough of hate
To know that for destruction ice
Is also great
And would suffice.

—Robert Frost

1. Edit the sentence for punctuation, spelling, and capitalization.

when frost returned from england prominmant publishers backed his work and americas most pretegous Universities invite him to teach in there schools

2. Write an endnote for page 83 of the book *Frost: A Literary Life Reconsidered,* by William H. Pritchard. The book was written in 1984 and published by Oxford University Press in New York.

3. Combine these sentences for better readability.

Robert Frost was born in San Francisco.
He lived there until he was 12.
His father died.
Then he moved to Massachusetts.

4. What is **dialogue**?

5. What does the word **rued** mean?

Dust of Snow

The way a crow
Shook down on me
The dust of snow
From a hemlock tree

Has given my heart
A change of mood
And saved some part
Of a day I had rued.

by Robert Frost

1. Edit the sentence.

at age twenty six frost moved to a farm near derry new hampshire where he got to know the inhabitents of rurel new england

2. What is an **appositive phrase**?

3. Write three attributes of historical fiction.

4. Circle the adverb in each sentence. Draw an arrow to show what word it modifies.

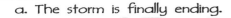

a. The storm is finally ending.

b. The drifts are quite deep.

c. It almost never snows this hard.

d. I will shovel walks tomorrow.

5. Read this stanza of Robert Frost's well-known poem **Stopping By the Woods on a Snowy Evening**.

He gives his harness bells a shake
To ask if there is some mistake.
The only other sound's the sweep
Of easy wind and downy flake.

Imagine the sound: the sweep of easy wind and downy flake. Would you hear the sound as you travel home? To which senses does Frost's description appeal? What kind of mood does the description create?

1. Define the word **embedded**.

Robert Frost's poetry has deeply embedded itself in the American imagination.

2. Add the ending -ing to each of the words.

a. dip   b. repel   c. reset
d. develop   e. train

3. Write three research questions you would ask when preparing a report about William Wordsworth's influence on Robert Frost's poetry.

4. Write a short note inviting someone to join you for an activity.

5. Read the invitation in Robert Frost's short poem *The Pasture*. What does his invitation mean to you?

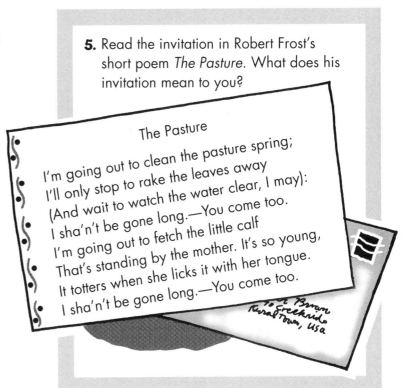

The Pasture

I'm going out to clean the pasture spring;
I'll only stop to rake the leaves away
(And wait to watch the water clear, I may):
I sha'n't be gone long.—You come too.
I'm going out to fetch the little calf
That's standing by the mother. It's so young,
It totters when she licks it with her tongue.
I sha'n't be gone long.—You come too.

Mending Wall

Something there is that doesn't love a wall,
That sends the frozen-ground-swell under it,
And spills the upper boulders in the sun,
And makes gaps even two can pass abreast.
The work of hunters is another thing:
I have come after them and made repair
Where they have left not one stone on a stone,
But they would have the rabbit out of hiding,
To please the yelping dogs. The gaps I mean,
No one has seen them made or heard them made,
But at spring mending-time we find them there.
I let my neighbor know beyond the hill;
And on a day we meet to walk the line
And set the wall between us once again.
We keep the wall between us as we go.
To each the boulders that have fallen to each.
And some are loaves and some so nearly balls
We have to use a spell to make them balance:
'Stay where you are until our backs are turned!'
We wear our fingers rough with handling them.
Oh, just another kind of outdoor game,
One on a side. It comes to little more:
There where it is we do not need the wall:
He is all pine and I am apple orchard.
My apple trees will never get across
And eat the cones under his pines, I tell him.
He only says, 'Good fences make good neighbors'.
Spring is the mischief in me, and I wonder
If I could put a notion in his head:
'Why do they make good neighbors? Isn't it
Where there are cows?
But here there are no cows.
Before I built a wall I'd ask to know
What I was walling in or walling out,
And to whom I was like to give offense.
Something there is that doesn't love a wall,
That wants it down.' I could say 'Elves' to him,
But it's not elves exactly, and I'd rather
He said it for himself. I see him there
Bringing a stone grasped firmly by the top
In each hand, like an old-stone savage armed.
He moves in darkness as it seems to me,
Not of woods only and the shade of trees.
He will not go behind his father's saying,
And he likes having thought of it so well
He says again, 'Good fences make good neighbors.'

by Robert Frost

Read

1. Describe each man's property.

2. The narrator says that mending walls is just another kind of outdoor game. What does he mean?

3. Explain the line, "We have to use a spell to make them balance."

4. Do the two men share a common philosophy about fences?

5. Think of a famous wall (the Berlin Wall, the Great Wall of China). What do you think walls symbolize? Compare the "fences" in Mr. Frost's poem with your perceptions of a wall.

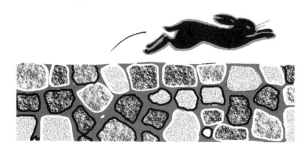

Write

Take a position. Do you believe that good fences make good neighbors? Support your opinion with facts and write a persuasive paragraph explaining your position.

1. Use proofreading marks for capitalization.

baron pierre de coubertin was the founder of the modern olympic games

2. Rewrite the sentence to make the meaning clear.

The coach told the gymnast that he should learn a new vault.

3. Circle the correctly spelled word.

forfeit   forfiet

4. Use the context to help you match the term to the correct definition.

____ the snatch   ____ the clean and jerk

a. Weightlifters lift the bar to arm's length above their head in one movement.

b. Weightlifters lift the bar to their shoulders, stand up straight, then jerk the bar to arm's length above their head.

5. In a single sentence describe the inspiration for the modern pentathlon.

A young French calvary officer of the 19th century was sent on horseback to deliver a message. He rode across the uneven terrain, through enemy lines, and was confronted by a soldier with his sword drawn. Challenged to a duel, the officer won, only to have his horse shot out from under him by another enemy soldier. After felling that soldier with a single shot, the officer ran on. He swam across a raging river, and then finally he delivered the message. So, legend has it, was born the modern pentathlon.

1. What should you do as you **revise** a piece of writing?

2. Add commas to this sentence.

Tug of war rugby polo lacrosse power boating and golf have all been Olympic events.

3. Correct the capitalization in this sentence.

The international olympic committee (ioc) is an international nonprofit organization.

4. Read the sentence describing one Olympic sport. Name the sport. Give synonyms for the underlined words.

Two <u>rivals</u> stand opposite each other and <u>feint</u>, lunge, parry, and riposte until one scores the required number of hits to win.

5. Use the two glossary entries to write a sentence that shows you understand the meaning of *slider* and *paddle* as used in the sport of luge.

Slider: A luge athlete, rarely called a luger.

Paddle: The action of accelerating the sled forward after the start, using spiked gloves to dig into the ice surface.

Name

1. Choose the correct sentence.

Either the players or the official _____ a time out.

○ signal   ○ signals

2. Circle the indirect object.

The official gave the hurdler a warning for leaving the block too soon.

3. Draw an illustration that shows a "Robin Hood".

In archery, the term "Robin Hood" refers to splitting the shaft of an arrow already in the target with another arrow.

4. Is this an effective opening for an article on Alberto Tomba? Why or why not?

Once the skis are on and the sunglasses readjusted, Italy's la Bomba (Alberto Tomba) clears his mind and scans the horizon . . . the light turns green, and off he goes.

5. Compare table tennis paddles of the past with today's paddles.

The first table tennis players used cigar-box lids for rackets and a carved champagne cork for a ball. Today, players use specially developed rubber-coated wooden and carbon-fibre rackets and a lightweight, hollow celluloid ball. Table tennis has become the world's largest participation sport, with 40 million competitive players worldwide and countless millions playing recreationally.

Table tennis debuted in the 1988 Olympic Games in Seoul.

Name

1. Cite the rule that explains why *Australian* is capitalized in this sentence.

The crowd stood respectfully as the trumpeter played the opening notes of the Australian national anthem.

2. Write the plurals.

Olympic competitor

passer-by

3. Edit the sentence.

the news casters enjoyed telling the athlets storys before the race began

4. How would you find out in which sport Chun competes?

Chun Lee-Kyung is one of only seven women to earn four or more career gold medals in the Winter Olympics.

5. Explain this statement: The Olympic sport of Judo represents an irony.

Judo means "the gentle way" in Japanese. Of course, it is derived in part from jujitsu, the hand-to-hand combat technique of ancient samurai warriors, and everything is relative. It is the only Olympic sport in which submission holds allow choking an opponent or breaking an arm.

Read

Over the roar of the crowd I strain to hear the first familiar notes of the melody. The crowd quiets as Old Glory starts its graceful ascent up the center pole and slowly unfurls in the evening breeze. The chill in the air transports me back to the pool. I stand shivering on the damp concrete and rubbing my hands on the rough surface of the starting block. I am nervous, but confident. Hours of practice have prepared me for this moment. Oblivious to the murmurs coming from the stands packed with spectators, I hear only the soft waves of water lapping at the edge of the pool. To my left and right I spot my opponents jumping, stretching, trying to loosen their muscles and calm their nerves. The best of the best are here and I am among them. Stepping up onto the starting block, I adjust my goggles, take a deep breath, and await the signal from the official starter.

"On your mark, Get set . . . "

The urgency of the orchestra and the swelling response of the crowd jolts me back to the present for a second.

"And the rockets' red glare . . . "

Tears of pride well up in my eyes. I once again see the crystal clear, blue-green lane ahead of me. One final turn of my head for a quick breath and, with the end in sight, I find the strength in my burning arms and legs to surge ahead. My fingers graze the wall and I emerge from the bubbles, gasping for air and spinning to see the results. The final strains of the music ring through the stadium and surge through my veins as I stand tall, watching the Stars and Stripes wave triumphant in the sky. My dream has come true.

---

1. What is a **flashback**?

2. Highlight sentences that represent flashbacks in this selection.

3. List a verb in the selection that appeals to each of the three senses: touch, hearing, and sight.

4. The second sentence represents another literary technique. What is it?

5. Describe the setting.

Write

Create a time line to show the actual sequence of events in the selection.

1. Define the noun **currency**.

2. Edit the sentence.

   Those whom collect currancy
   are generaly refered to
   as numismatists.

3. Explain why one currency converter's abbreviation for the British pound is GBP.

4. From your experience, give three specific examples of collectible currency.

   In recent years, there has been a dramatic
   surge in the demand for collectible currency.
   Prices have doubled and even tripled
   for certain examples. Both coins and
   paper money have experienced these
   sorts of gains.

5. Write four details that support the contention:

   Gold-dust is a desirable currency.

For more than four-hundred years, the Akan people of Ghana in West Africa used a currency based on tiny grains of gold called gold-dust. This very desirable currency made the Akan a valued trading partner to North African traders who crossed the Sahara Desert by camel caravan and to sea-faring Europeans who arrived on Africa's Atlantic Coast in ships laden with goods.

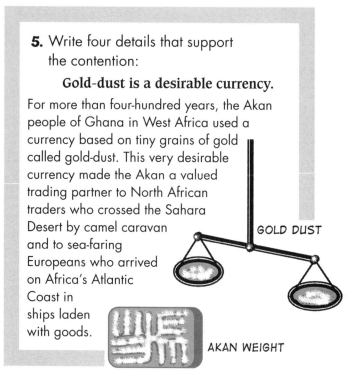

GOLD DUST

AKAN WEIGHT

1. Define the following homonyms.

   cent   scent

2. Edit the sentence.

   Foriegn traders did not want to spend
   hours negotiting every transaction
   with waits and scales.

3. Fact or opinion?

   It is possible to buy a house,
   a ticket, or even a pair of shoes
   without ever meeting the seller
   face-to-face or passing money
   from one hand to another.

4. Read the table to determine the number of Euro you would receive for $250 U.S. dollars.

DOLLARS
bucks
lettuce $
money
beans
bread   scratch   MOOLA   capital   dough

5. Take notes to remind yourself how collectible currency is valued.

   Collectible currency is judged on
   several factors. Some factors are based
   on subjective appearance, such as
   coloration, centering, finish, and wear.
   Other factors are more objective: date
   issued, series, mint/printing location,
   ink colors, number issued, and rarity in
   the market.

U.S. $1	YEN	EURO	CAN $	U.K.£	AU $	SWISS FRANC
	120.6250	0.7738	1.1769	0.5095	1.2764	1.2476

U.S. CURRENCY CONVERSION CHART

1. Edit the rules.

Never lie Valuble posessions down.
moniter belongings carefully.

2. Underline the complete subject.
Circle the simple subject.

The capacity to convert perishable commodities into money provides a powerful incentive for people to produce more than they need

3. In nonfiction writing what is a **thesis**?

4. Write several sentences describing the advantages and disadvantages of using the **handa** as your currency.

The handa is a solid copper currency used in the Congo in Africa. It is an x-shaped object approximately nine by six inches.

5. What are the basic tools numismatists use as they study and collect coins?

HOW TO BE A NUMISMATIST

The numismatist needs some basic equipment and training. First, you need a magnifying glass, ruler, and a bright white light. These will help you assess size and texture, as well as spot imperfections. A pricing

guide is available at nearly any bookstore and it will point out the differences between specimens. Additional information can be found on websites and in newsgroups all over the Internet covering all sorts of different collecting focuses.

---

1. List four important requirements for a good currency.

2. In which situation would you skim the guide?
- ○ you need specific details
- ○ you want general ideas

3. Is the U.S. paper dollar part of a commodity money system?

Under a commodity money system, the objects used as money have intrinsic value, i.e., they have value beyond their use as money.

4. List a synonym and an antonym for each word.

buy

request

courtesy

5. Alphabetize this list of international currencies.

INTERNATIONAL CURRENCIES		
LEK, ALBANIA	DALASIA, GAMBIA	KUNA, CROATIA
PESO, MEXICO	RUPEE, INDIA	KROON, ESTONIA
REAL, BRAZIL	RIAL, QATAR	EURO, EUROPE
LEVA, BULGARIA	DINAR, IRAQ	QUETZAL, GUATEMALA
KORUNA, CZECH	TAKA, BANGLADESH	RUPIAH, INDONESIA
BIRR, ETHIOPIA	RINGGIT, MALAYSIA	KWACHA, ZAMBIA

Read

Starting in the 1990s, several European countries interested in coordinating economic and fiscal policies formed the European Monetary Union (EMU). The EMU was a major step for those who committed to it. The members agreed to phase out their national currencies and introduce a new regional currency. On January 1, 2002, 300 million Europeans in 12 countries began using the *euro*. Germans gave up the deutschmark, the French bid adieu to the franc, and the other members also began to discontinue their currencies. On January 1, 2007, a 13th member, Slovenia, also joined in and replaced the tolar with the euro. Other European Union member countries may also introduce the euro in the future.

The euro is similar in value and denomination to the U.S. dollar. The symbol of the euro (€) was inspired by the Greek letter Epsilon. Euro notes are valued at 5, 10, 20, 50, 100, 200, and 500. Unlike the dollar, the euro does not have a one-euro bill. Instead, there are one-euro and two-euro coins. Euro bills also differ from American dollars because they are brightly colored and vary in size depending on their value, with the smallest denomination in the smallest size.

The introduction of the euro has eased travel and commerce within Europe. Travelers used to have to exchange money at every border. Now, they can use euro coins and bills in every country that belongs to the EMU. Long-time residents are still adjusting to paying €3 instead of 41 schillings for a cup of Viennese coffee or €150 instead of 300,000 lira for a pair of Italian leather shoes. But the new currency makes traveling in Europe and understanding price levels much easier for tourists and business people. Since its introduction in 2002, this regional currency has been a tremendous success and has brought the countries and people of Europe closer together than ever before.

€ 3
(41 shillings)

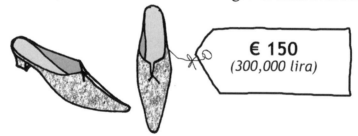

€ 150
(300,000 lira)

---

1. What is a **fiscal** policy?

2. Why was forming the European Monetary Union a **major** step?

3. How are euro bills different than U.S. dollar bills?

4. Summarize the benefits of using the euro.

Write

Write an advertising slogan for the idea of one regional currency. Use what you have learned by reading the encyclopedia article to make your slogan realistic.

1. What phrase does this group of letters represent?

ABCDEFGHJMOP (HINT: WHAT LETTERS ARE MISSING?)

2. Anagrams are words that have the same letters—only the letters are rearranged. Find an anagram for each word.

canoe   **reserved**   **robed**

3. What one word can be matched to the other five to form a phrase, expression, or compound word?

trial   over   double   dinner   out

4. Read the clue and figure out the two-word phrase. Both words in the phrase begin with the same letter.

• instructions at intersection
• wild, risk-taking characters

5. Using the nine letters make as many words as you can with four or more letters. Give yourself 1 point for every 4-letter word, 2 points for every 5-letter word, 3 points for every 6-letter word, and 5 points for any longer words.

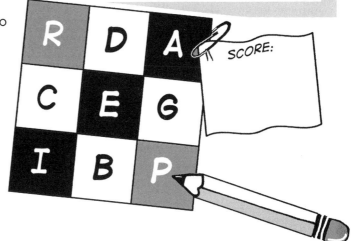

SCORE:

1. Add punctuation to this quotation.

Seneca said Human affairs are like a chess game only those who do not take it seriously can be called good players.

2. Use the context to define the term **checkmate**.

The ultimate goal in the game of chess is to win by trapping your opponent's king, a move called checkmate.

3. Why would you use the **castling move**?

Castling is a special defensive maneuver. It is the only time in the game when more than one piece may be moved during a turn. The move was invented in the 1500s to help speed up the game and to balance the offense and defense.

4. Use proofreading marks to edit the sentence.

the first offisial world chess champion wilhelm steinitz clamed his title in 1886

5. Read this passage about chess.

Today, chess is one of the world's most popular sports, played by an estimated 605 million people worldwide in clubs, online, by correspondence (mail and e-mail), in tournaments (amateur and professional), and informally. It is advocated as a way of enhancing mental prowess.

Do you think it possible to enhance mental prowess by playing a game? Write a thesis statement that states your position and support it with examples.

1. Edit the sentence.

In the early 1930s alfred butts created a boardless game he called lexico that was the predecesser to another of his games scrabble.

2. Name the tone of the player's comment.

"Well, it is impossible for me to believe that you would stoop to such a level! Humpf! I needed that space for my next turn, and now you have ruined my play. I don't believe that I will ever again agree to a game of Scrabble with such despicable players."

3. Complete the analogy.

letters: utterance :: notes : _____

4. Rewrite this fragment as a complete sentence.

Perusing the board to find a play.

5. A Scrabble player must be able to recognize when an opponent is trying to play an unacceptable word. Cross out the words on the board below that are not correctly spelled.

1. Would you like the **monopoly on miscues**? Why or why not?

2. Add parentheses to make the meaning clear.

World records are maintained for the longest game played in a treehouse 286 hours, underground 100 hours, in a bathtub 99 hours and upside-down 36 hours.

3. Edit the sentence.

Most foriegn editions of monopoly adopt their own currancy and property names—for example BOARDWALK becomes mayfair in england rue de la paix in france and schlossallee in germany.

4. Instructions for many MONOPOLY games are available as PDF files. How would you access them?

5. Review the facts and then write an opening sentence for an informative article about the game Monopoly.

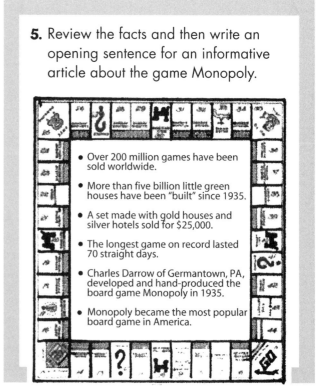

- Over 200 million games have been sold worldwide.
- More than five billion little green houses have been "built" since 1935.
- A set made with gold houses and silver hotels sold for $25,000.
- The longest game on record lasted 70 straight days.
- Charles Darrow of Germantown, PA, developed and hand-produced the board game Monopoly in 1935.
- Monopoly became the most popular board game in America.

LANGUAGE PRACTICE

CROSSWORD QUIZZER

Read

Read the clues and complete the puzzle using the words in the word bank.

Across

2. A list of terms and their meanings
4. More than one
5. "He had the heart of a lion," for example
11. Buzz, bark, or thud, for example
12. A type of literature
13. Exaggeration or overstatement
14. An invented story
15. A word that is written and pronounced the same way as another, but which has a different meaning
16. Educated guess or friendly argument, for example

Down

1. A reflection of the writer's attitude toward the subject
3. "Dashing Don drove drowsy Daisy downtown," for example
6. Biggest, funniest, or saddest, for example
7. "She was as happy as a clam," for example
8. An introductory statement
9. A word that joins together sentences, clauses, phrases, or words
10. The end

Word Bank

tone
glossary
alliteration
plural
metaphor
superlative
simile
preamble
conjunction
conclusion
onomatopoeia
genre
hyperbole
fiction
homonym
oxymoron

Write

Do you like crossword puzzles? Make two lists:
one list of reasons that doing a crossword puzzle is time well-spent, and
one list of reasons that working a crossword puzzle is a waste of time.

Name

1. Explain the capitalization guideline for the closing in a letter.

2. Do you agree with poet Sandra Cisneros? Why or why not?

   Letter writing is "listening inside my heart to how I'm being affected by the outside world."

3. Edit the sentence.

   amazeingly Ive read your book four times and learn something new everytime.

4. Which thesis statement is most persuasive and why?

   • Some television programs have really bad effects on young children.

   • Violent television shows cause violent behavior and nightmares in young children.

5. Explain the difference between the heading of a friendly letter and the heading of a business letter.

Feb. 12, 2007

Dear Aunt Betty,

Antiques and Collectibles
518 Old Hickory Blvd., Bellevue, TX 97218
tel: 555-6600; toll free: 1-800-555-6700   fax: 1-555-8392

George Parquette
Ye Olde Junque Yard
2020 Harbor Rd.
Pinto, TX 97654

January 23, 2007

Dear Sir:

Name

1. Classify the letters below as friendly or business.
   a. thank-you note to Aunt Maria
   b. complaint about fading to jeans' maker
   c. compliment to frozen pizza maker
   d. apology to neighbor for breaking window

2. Use the subordinate clause in a sentence.
   before I was halfway through

3. True or false?
   If the first line of the body of a letter is indented, all other paragraphs in the letter must also be indented.

4. Address this envelope to the principal of your school. Be sure to include a return address.

5. Sequence the steps for writing a letter to the editor.
   • Explain how your evidence supports your claim.
   • Present evidence in a logical sequence.
   • Identify your purpose.
   • Conclude by reaffirming your claim.
   • State your central claim clearly.

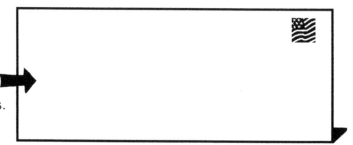

1. Give two different meanings for each word.

   a. letter

   b. note

   c. stamp

2. Add appropriate punctuation to this salutation for a business letter.

   Dear Dr. Crawford

3. Explain the pun.

   Claude Severely is an ex-lion tamer.

4. What is the difference between summarizing and paraphrasing?

5. President Dwight D. Eisenhower began writing to Prime Minister Winston Churchill on February 2, 1953, just two weeks after Eisenhower's inauguration. The private correspondence continued regularly throughout the time Churchill and Eisenhower were in office.

   a. Why would this private correspondence be valuable to these two men?

   b. Explain this line Eisenhower wrote to Churchhill:

   It would be difficult for me to find a single line in your letter with which I disagree, even if I were minded to look for such an opportunity.

1. Explain the difference between **stationery** and **stationary**.

2. Circle the correctly spelled closings.

   Luv,   Your firend,

   Sincerely,   Affectionatly,

   Yours truely,   Your neice,

3. Complete the analogy.

   letter : epistle :: paper :

4. Explain the meaning of the underlined word.

   Chester hates water. He hates sunshine. He hates sand. Therefore, his friends were <u>confounded</u> when he wrote a letter to the editor promoting development of a new beach.

5. Abraham Lincoln wrote to a friend:

"Looking into the glass it struck me what an ugly man I was. The fact grew on me and I made up my mind I must be the ugliest man in the world."

A. Lincoln

Explain how this statement might be considered **hyperbole**.

Read

Dear Mr. Frost:

I hope that this letter finds you well and in good health. We've never met, but I feel as if we are kindred spirits. After reading "A Boy's Will" and hearing about your recent participation in President Kennedy's inauguration, I was inspired to learn more about your poetry and your life. Though I am a young man who is just on the brink of my writing career and you are an accomplished Pulitzer Prize winner–four times over no less—we actually have much in common.

Like you, I was born in California and eventually found my way to New England. We also both spent time at Harvard. I am trying desperately to finish my studies, a feat that I understand you never officially completed, having been pulled away by family responsibilities. You have since been recognized, of course, with an astounding 26 honorary degrees and have taught at numerous prestigious institutions including Amherst College, the University of Michigan, Dartmouth, and even Harvard itself. I can only dream of such honors and opportunities.

I understand that you traveled across the Atlantic many times and spent three years in England early in your career. I have traveled to England, too, but I've gone only once and stayed for just a few months. Perhaps one day I can return to visit Oxford or, if my dreams really come true, I'll have the opportunity, as you did, to meet influential poets and creative minds from around the world at the World Congress of Writers.

Having taken too much of your time already, I will close with a thank-you and a pledge. Thank you for being an inspiration to me and to all aspiring poets. As I embark on my artistic journey, I will endeavor to find "a time to talk" and, as you have done, to take the "road less traveled by".

Best regards from a kindred spirit,

1. What is **a kindred spirit**?

2. Record the biographical information about Robert Frost included in the letter as if you were taking notes for a report.

3. Many expressions that we use every day originated in literature. We use the words and phrases in everyday speech; however, we are often unaware that we are "borrowing" them from famous writers. Explain how this statement relates to the pledge the letter writer makes.

Write

Write a letter to a poet or writer who has influenced you. Be sure to include biographical information that shows you know something about the person.

Note: A national program called _Letters About Literature_, sponsored by The Center for the Book in the Library of Congress awards prizes each year for letters written by high school students to famous authors. Email lettersaboutlit@epix.net for further information.

1. Combine the sentences for readability and flow.

- The American Civil War was a separatist conflict.
- The war was between the U.S. Federal government and the Confederate States of America.
- Eleven states seceded from the U.S. to form the Confederate States of America.

2. What is wrong with this sentence?

General Lee bearly managed to escape back to Virginia.

3. Define each of these words.

secession

casualties

confederate

4. What is the plural form of **crisis**?

To the
Army and Navy of the Union

When Johnny Comes Marching Home
⌘
Introduced by
Gilmore's Band
❖
words and music by
Louis Lambert
Boston
Published by Henry Tolman & Co,
291 Washington Street
1863

5. Look at the reproduction of the sheet music cover and tell
   a. the title of the song
   b. who first performed the music
   c. to whom it was dedicated
   d. what year the copyright was recorded and where

1. Dissect the word **reinforcement** into prefixes, root, and suffix. Give the meaning of each.

2. List two details that support the contention:

There was a strong correlation between the number of plantations in a region and the degree of support for secession.

3. Edit the sentence.

The union lead by president abraham lincoln opossed the expantion of slavry and rejectted any right of seccession.

4. Is a **fanatical** belief one that is carefully thought out and calmly studied?

5. Tell what you know about the map after reading this notation made on the corner.

MAP
of the
FIELD OF SHILOH
near Pittsburgh Landing, Tennessee
showing the position of the
U.S. Forces under the Command
of Maj.Gen. **U.S. Grant** U.S. Vol.
and
Maj. Gen. **D.C. Buell** U.S. Vol.
on the 6th and 7th of April, 1862
Surveyed under the direction of
Col. Geo. Thomas, Chief of Top. Eng**
Dept. of the Mississippi
Scale: 1 inch to 1,200 feet

1. Add punctuation to make the meaning clear.

Union advantages in geography manpower industry finance political organization and transportation overwhelmed the Confederacy

2. Stephen C. Foster was a composer during the Civil War. Paraphrase this verse from his song "Beautiful Dreamer".

Beautiful dreamer, queen of my song,
List while I woo thee with soft melody;
Gone are the cares of life's busy throng,
Beautiful dreamer, awake unto me!

3. What is an **ode**?

4. Paraphrase this statement in South Carolina's argument for secession.

"We maintain that in every compact between two or more parties, the obligation is mutual."

5. Read this note. Use the context to guess the definition of **Casus Belli**. Then use a dictionary to see whether you were correct.

Fort Sumter

Date: April 12, 1861 - April 9, 1865
Location: Principally in the Southern United States
Result: Union victory; Reconstruction; Slavery abolished
Casus belli: Confederate attack on Fort Sumter

1. Reorder this sentence for clarity.

Before Lincoln took office, seven states declared their secession from the Union and established a new government, the Confederate States of America on February 9, 1861.

2. Name three keywords you might use to read about Civil War conflicts.

3. Have you ever intervened in a conflict? What does it mean to **intervene**?

4. Identify the contradiction in this time line entry.

5. Categorize the subtopics.

A. Civil War Issues
B. Major Battles
C. Aftermath of Civil War

- Abolition
- Antietam
- Reconstruction
- Slavery
- Pickett's Charge
- Shiloh
- 13th Amendment
- Franklin

July, 1776	August, 1776	Sept, 1776

The American Colonies declare independence from English rule with the adoption of *The Declaration of Independence*. The document, written largely by Thomas Jefferson, declares all men are created equal. Jefferson and many framers of the revolutionary paper are slaveholders.

Read

July 23, 1861

I've decided to write a bit, to take my mind off my aching feet. The humidity is unbearable, not to mention the mosquitoes, and I'm nursing blisters sustained during our hurried and shameful retreat from Manassas. The march was made harder by the shift in mood and the panicked, stunned spectators who blocked the roads after fleeing their picnic spots around the battlefield. Yesterday's confrontation weighs heavy on the minds of my fellow soldiers. It no longer seems that I can plan to be home at Christmas time to enjoy Gram's roasted duck. The Confederates have come to fight, and fight they did at Bull Run. Our numbers were far greater and we made a good start, but then the battle shifted as we crested Henry House Hill. The Confederates were waiting for us and we lost our confidence. The battle lines broke; we began to flee. I saw hundreds fleeing. Many were taken prisoner and others suffered a far worse fate than that. I am grateful to be alive and, save my miserable feet, uninjured.

The days ahead seem gray, uncertain. There are rumors that the Army of Northeastern Virginia will be disbanded or merged with another force. If Brigadier General McDowell is replaced, as we are certain he will be, I pray for a cunning, yet sympathetic leader. My fellow soldiers and I are true of heart, but green as saplings in the spring when it comes to the ways of war. We have not yet been hardened by battle, though having survived Bull Run, we can claim one notch on our belt. One thing is certain—we face a formidable foe in our Confederate counterparts. They were not the ragtag band of rebels we expected to rout. They were trained and they fought with a passion that the Union lacks. Tomorrow will bring another day, another march, and another step, no matter how small, toward the end of this ugly war.

1. What assumptions can you make about the character who wrote this journal entry?

2. Although the entry is informal the writer uses "formal" language—**nursing blisters sustained during . . . .** Explain possible reasons for the author's choice of words.

3. Explain the use of the phrases:
   a. "save my miserable feet"   b. one notch in our belts

4. What literary device is used in the final sentence? Do you think it is effectively used?

Write

List the attributes of historical fiction. Does this journal entry represent legitimate historical fiction?

1. Correct the spelling.

Antartica

emergancy

shedule

2. What mode would you use to write a travel brochure for a South Pacific island?

3. What is a **destination**?

4. Add punctuation to this quotation.

The speaker enthusiastically advocated international travel asserting all who travel overseas learn quickly that understanding and tolerance are fostered by common experience.

5. Critique this description. Does it have a positive appeal? Would you visit Cabo San Lucas after reading it? Why or why not?

Day 2: Along the west embankment of Cabo's modest bay—one of Mexico's deepest natural ports—hop on one of the white-painted water taxis for a 15-minute ride to Playa del Amante. This wide, pristine, golden expanse of sand is a marine preserve, so you won't be badgered by beach-blanket peddlers. Just off the southeast end of the beach lies a series of coral-encrusted rocks suitable for snorkeling, where the Sea of Cortez showcases colorful schools of fish.

1. Where would you find the most accurate and timely information about travel to Aleppo?

a. U.S. State Department Web site

b. Promotional brochure from Syrian Arab Republic Board of Tourism

c. Discount travel Web site

2. Edit the sentence.

All customers must carry goverment issued identification with him at all times and may be ask to show identification during boarding.

3. Enhance the meaning of this phrase with an explicit verb and descriptive phrases.

The traveler boarded the train.

4. What is a **participle**?

5. Paraphrase this warning.

Extreme care should be exercised when touring Iceland's numerous natural attractions, which include glaciers, volcanic craters, lava fields, ice caves, hot springs, boiling mud pots, geysers, waterfalls, and glacial rivers.

There are few warning signs or barriers to alert travelers to potential hazards.

High winds and icy conditions can exacerbate the hidden dangers of Iceland's attractions.

Several tourists are scalded each year because they get too close to an erupting geyser, or because they step into hot springs or mud pots.

splurp

1. Fact or opinion?

Alliance Airlines is the perfect choice for leisure groups, family reunions, or any groups traveling together.

2. Dissect the word. Give meanings for the prefix, root, and suffix.

transportation

3. Edit the sentence.

How can I chose between barcelona paris and vienna.

4. Do you think the two men hold a common opinion about the value of travel? Why or why not?

St. Augustine said, "The world is a book, and those who do not travel read only a page."

Robert Louis Stevenson said, "I travel not to go anywhere, but to go. I travel for travel's sake."

5. Explain a reason behind each of these important tips for traveling.

1. Make sure you have a signed, valid passport and visas, if required.

2. Familiarize yourself with the local laws and customs of the countries where you are traveling.

3. Do not wear conspicuous clothing and expensive jewelry, or carry excessive amounts of money or credit cards.

4. Leave a copy of your itinerary with family or friends at home.

1. Edit the sentence

While vacationing Sam caught a marlin fishing from the yacht.

2. Choose the correct word.

The woman felt _____ when on the plane.

indisposed   indigenous

3. What would you find in a **gazetteer**?

4. The U.S. State Department issued this travel advisory for travelers going to Barundi, Bangladesh. Summarize its message.

The security situation has stabilized in much of the country, but the risk of sudden outbreaks of armed violence, acts of banditry, and cross-border incursion by rebel groups remains. Private Americans should exercise caution and maintain security awareness at all times.

5. Use the airport code information chart to answer the questions.

a. What is the airport code for Dyce Airport?

b. What country is home to ADD?

c. If you want to fly to Almaty what is your destination airport?

City	State/Country	City Airport	Airport Code
AALBORG	Denmark	Aalborg	AAL
ABERDEEN	United Kingdom	Dyce Airport	ABZ
ABU DHABI	United Arab Emirates	Abu Dhabi International	AUH
ADDIS ABABA	Ethiopia	Bole Airport	ADD
ALMATY	Kazakhstan	Alma Ata Airport	ALA

TRAVEL TIPS

Read

Even before you board the plane for an international flight or cruise into international waters, you'll realize that traveling abroad is more complex than visiting another domestic location. Months ahead of your trip you must apply for a passport or check your existing passport to make sure it has not expired. If it is your first time getting a passport, you will have to complete an application, have your picture taken, and present identification such as a birth certificate or driver's license. A passport is required to enter a foreign country and is a crucial document to identify your citizenship when you are traveling abroad.

Another step in preparing for international travel is making sure that your vaccinations and immunizations are up to date. You may need to be vaccinated to protect against diseases such as Tuberculosis, Hepatitis A and B, or Yellow Fever. Your doctor may also recommend that you take medication during your trip, particularly if you are headed to an area where malaria has not yet been eradicated.

In addition to preparing your passport and consulting your doctor, it is a good idea to familiarize yourself with the location of the U.S. Embassy or consulate nearest your destination. Embassies and consulates provide general information about travel conditions and issue travel warnings if there are concerns related to crime, terrorism, or natural disasters. Travelers may also need to rely on an Embassy or Consulate if they need assistance, such as a replacement passport, a repatriation loan, or even a birth certificate, while they are abroad. Information about U.S. Embassy and consulate locations can be found on www.state.gov.

So, before you plan your trip to Moscow, Bangkok, or Ouagadougou, remember to prepare your passport, update your immunizations and vaccinations, and identify the closest embassy or consulate. Bon Voyage!

Mark each statement ***true*** or ***false***. Then justify your answer with details from the memo.

1. Domestic and international travel are two names for the same thing.

2. This travel memo was written for a general audience worldwide.

3. Immunizations required for travel may vary depending on the traveler's destination.

4. International travel requires little advance planning.

5. A government embassy is a good place to get funds in case of an emergency.

Write

Imagine that you are planning an international study trip. Pick a destination. Make a list of the things you should do before the trip. Prioritize the list.

MONDAY WEEK 25 _____ LANGUAGE PRACTICE

1. Define the following words. Use what you know about prefixes and suffixes to help.
- **reunification**
- **subsidies**
- **unemployment**

2. Define the noun **bias** as it relates to public opinion.

3. Which statement is more meaningful to you? Why?

The country of Germany is slightly smaller than the state of Montana.

Germany has a total area of 357,021 sq. km.

4. Add punctuation to the sentence.

As Europes largest economy and second most populous nation germany is a key member of the continents economic political and defense organizations

5. Explain this German proverb. What literary device does the comparison represent?

Die Lügen sind wie Schneebälle: je weiter man sie fortwälzt, desto größer werden sie.

(Lies are like snowballs: the farther they roll, the bigger they get.)

TUESDAY WEEK 25 _____ LANGUAGE PRACTICE

1. Explain the difference in meaning:
beside   besides

2. Write the possessive form of countries.
The _____ treaty . . .

3. True or false?
Scanning is a good way to evaluate information as you read.

4. Combine the sentences. Make sure that the verb tenses agree.

The Berlin wall separated the city into two parts for more than 28 years.

At first the wall is a system of barbed wire entanglement and fences dividing the city.

Concrete blocks and steel girders were added.

East Germans are not allowed free travel to the West until 1989.

JFK

On June 26, 1963, President John F. Kennedy delivered a speech in the shadow of the Berlin Wall. As he paid tribute to the spirit of Berliners, he proclaimed, "Ich bin ein Berliner" (I am a Berliner).

Twenty-four years later, President Ronald Reagan appeared at the Berlin Wall. He spoke passionately about the advance of human liberty and challenged Soviet leader Mikhail Gorbachev to tear down the wall and commit to change.

5. Think about audience and purpose of the two famous speeches. Do you think Kennedy and Reagan had similar purposes? Did their audience extend beyond the people of Berlin? Explain.

1. *Healthy* is to *robust* as *inane* is to _____.

2. Edit the sentence.

former president holtz koehler lives in the capital city of germany frankfurt

3. What is the **theme** of a story?

4. Johann Wolfgang von Goethe, German poet and one of the world's masters of literature, wrote:

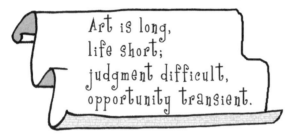

Art is long,
life short;
judgment difficult,
opportunity transient.

Paraphrase the quotation and tell whether you agree with the sentiment.

5. Write a topic sentence that describes the division of German territory at the end of World War II.

_____

_____

- Germany had been divided into four occupation zones.
- 1949—French, British, and American zones (and West Berlin) form the Federal Republic of Germany.
- Soviet zone forms the German Democratic Republic (including East Berlin), same year.
- February 1945—Pomerania and Silesia, and southern half of East Prussia, are annexed by Poland.
- Northern half of East Prussia is annexed by the Soviet Union.

1. Rewrite to make the pronoun reference clear.

The Chancellor loved public speaking, and that helped boost her popularity.

2. Rewrite the sentence, changing the tense of the verb from past to present perfect.

Children enjoyed the Grimm Brothers' famous tales.

3. What is an **antecedent**?

4. Read the notes. Tell why Germany's telephone system has excellent worldwide service.

General Assessment of Germany's Phone System

- intensive capital expenditures
- formerly backward system
- connected by networks of fiber-optic cable
- extensive land and undersea cable facilities
- earth stations in satellite systems

5. Read the explanation, then explain the evolution of the German phrase *die Wende*.

The term "die Wende" has taken on a new meaning. Before 1990, it simply meant "the turnaround". Today the term is used to refer to events that led up to the German reunification. It has taken on a cultural connotation encompassing the time and the events in the GDR that brought about a "turnaround" in German history.

Read

As Europe's largest economy and second most populous nation, Germany remains a key member of the continent's economic, political, and defense organizations.

1. How many miles from Berlin to Stuttgart?

2. Name the major rivers of Germany.

3. What countries border Germany? What bodies of water?

4. Why is Germany important to the continent of Europe?

Write

Compare the size of Germany with the size of your country in a way that makes the comparison meaningful.

1. What is an **autobiography**?

2. Write an antonym for each word.

continuous

eventually

survive

persevere

3. Edit the sentence.

While living in rocky ridge missouri laura wilder edited and writes columns for the missouri ruralist.

4. Laura Ingalls Wilder earned her teaching degree when she was 15. Could you learn from a 15-year-old teacher? List arguments for and against young educators.

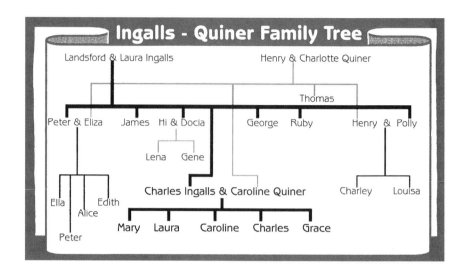

Ingalls - Quiner Family Tree

5. How many *maternal* aunts and uncles did Laura Ingalls have?

1. How would you change this thesis statement to make it more specific?

Laura Ingalls Wilder shared her pioneer experiences with generations.

2. Underline the complete predicate. Circle the simple predicate.

Following in the pioneer footsteps of their familes, Laura and Almanzo struggled to establish homes first in South Dakota and later in Minnesota.

3. Combine the two sentences.

• **Laura's sister Mary lost her eyesight when she was 15.**

• **As a result of a stroke, Mary lost her eyesight.**

4. What does **homesteading** mean?

5. After reading the passage below, circle the adjectives that describe Laura Ingalls Wilder.

FRAIL   resourceful   indolent   pessimistic   enduring   persistent

Laura Ingalls Wilder was disappointed when she couldn't find a publisher for her autobiography, *Pioneer Girl*, so she rewrote a section of the book and called it *Little House in the Big Woods*. It was published in 1932 when she was 65 years old. Laura continued to write books about her family, finishing her 8-volume series in 1943.

1. Add commas to the sentence.

Laura Elizabeth Ingalls was born February 7 1867 the second daughter of Charles and Caroline Ingalls in the big woods 7 miles north of Pepin Wisconsin.

2. Circle the words that are spelled correctly.

uncomplicated   **trespasing**

technque   **manageable**

3. True or false?

Place quotation marks around the exact words quoted.

4. Rewrite the sentence in the future tense.

After they stopped farming, Laura and her husband Almanzo took care of a pet bulldog, a Rocky Mountain burro, and milk goats.

5. The Laura Ingalls Wilder Award honors an author or illustrator whose books, published in the United States, have made, over a period of years, a substantial and lasting contribution to literature for children. Think of an author that you believe will make a lasting contribution to literature for children. Write three reasons you think the author should win the Laura Ingalls Wilder Award.

Laurence Yep was the 2005 winner of the **Laura Ingalls Wilder Award**. After 30 years of writing, his 55 titles include "Dragonwings", "The Rainbow People", and "The Lost Garden". The selection committee noted, "Across a variety of literary genres, Laurence Yep explores the universal dilemma of the cultural outsider."

Which author would you choose to win this award and why?

1. Laura Ingalls Wilder documented the hardships of frontier life in America. What hardships exist in your community? Write a paragraph documenting surviving one. (Your writing doesn't have to be serious. You may think of "funny" hardships.)

2. What is a **glossary**? Where will you find one?

3. Edit this bibliography entry.

Laura Ingalls Wilder, Little House on the prairie: (HarperCollins, 1935).

4. Choose the correct words.

a. (**Leave, Let**) us go to the movie.

b. Some vistors who (**could have, could of**) seen the exhibit, (**passed, past**) on the opportunity.

5. If you arrived in Pepin on Saturday night, September 9, would you be able to take part in the Old Tyme Fiddle Contest?

Come and Celebrate Laura Ingalls Wilder Day
On the **140th** Anniversary of Her Birth

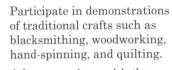

Participate in demonstrations of traditional crafts such as blacksmithing, woodworking, hand-spinning, and quilting.

On Saturday night we continue with the candlelight traditional crafts demonstrations accompanied by a bonfire & traditional musical performances. The festival's activities culminate on Sunday afternoon with the Grand Parade.

The 6th Annual Fiddle Contest highlights the entertainment on Saturday afternoon. Old Tyme Fiddle Contest Registration from 10:00 to 3:00 p.m.; Contest from 3:30 to 6:00 p.m.

Read

Many others like Laura Ingalls Wilder remember their childhoods and record stories for future generations.

Remembering my mother, Viola Phillips Sutter . . .

What an adjustment Mother must have made! She married a farmer and moved to the prairie. Her piano and a few treasures were loaded onto a wagon and she waved good-bye to her family. Within four years she had three children, and she lived in a house with no electricity or phone. She had to carry water in and out, make her own soap, and begin to learn how to cook. With a shy smile she admitted that when she was married she knew how to make only angel food cakes, white house muffins, divinity—and little else! It must have been a relief when she moved near another large family. Their two elementary-aged girls played house with Mother's two baby girls—my sister and me. The capable mother of the family helped cook for threshers when they came to our place, asking, in return, that Mother teach her girls to play the piano . . .

Mother would set hens on fertile eggs, both turkeys' and chickens', and struggled raising little broods of chicks. When a storm was threatening, we were all summoned to herd the old hens and their babies into small coops. Those turkeys were largely the means of having new school clothes and Christmas gifts during those Depression years . . .

I believe Mother taught me to be caring to others, to make do with what was at hand, to be conservative, and never to compromise my principles.

—Betty Bagley

1. After reading the memoir entry, describe Viola Sutter. What do you know about her? What kind of a person was she?

2. What can you tell about the place and time where Viola Sutter lived with her young family?

3. Laura Ingalls Wilder wrote about her childhood in the Big Woods of Wisconsin. How are the memories shared by Betty Bagley like the *Little House* stories? What qualities are reflected in the stories told by the two authors?

4. What is a memoir? Do you have to be near the end of your life to write a memoir?

Write

Write about a person who has taught you something. Describe the person in a way that lets readers know about his or her values and the context of the lesson you learned.

1. What's wrong with this definition? Fix it!

Castanets—Percussion instruments consisting of small wooden clappers that are struck together. It is widely used to accompany Spanish dancing.

2. Whose point of view?

I headed for Nashville at age 16 with my guitar over my shoulder and a song in my head.

3. Choose the correctly spelled word.

morgage   **mortgage**

4. Musicians interpret words in special ways. Write the definition a musician would use for these terms.

piano (adjective)

pitch (noun)

5. Personify music as you write a sentence or two about something music does.

Music speaks what cannot be expressed
Soothes the mind and gives it rest,
Heals the heart and makes it whole,
Flows from heaven to the soul.
Music washes away from the soul
the dust of everyday life.
Berthold Auerbach

1. Edit the sentence.

the flutest, went to the oberlin music conservatory, to learn to play the obo.

2. Which is correct?

Her phrasing improved (**alot, a lot**).

3. Lists three attributes of **punk rock**.

4. Take a position on this statement. Write three research questions you would investigate to find facts to support your position.

The process of making music is the reward.

1. _____

2. _____

3. _____

5. Check these song titles for capitalization.

1. *Face it Girl it's Over!*
2. Fable of the rose
3. Babe i'm Gonna leave you
4. B is for Barney
5. baa, baa black sheep

1. Explain the mistakes in this sentence.

> **People, whom are afraid of performing in front of audiences, do not become soloists.**

2. A crescendo is the dynamic effect of gradually growing louder, indicated in the musical score by the marking "<". Make these action words crescendo by choosing a "louder" verb.

> **run**
>
> **argue**

3. What is a **ballad**?

4. Explain what it means.

> I CAN'T GET THAT TUNE OUT OF MY HEAD!

5. Read this excerpt from a **New York Times** review. Summarize the review and tell whether you think the reviewer enjoyed the concert.

Theater & Arts   March 15-22

String players applied vibrato liberally, offering a warm, fuzzy opulence that sometimes thwarted precise articulation; the oboists and bassoonist projected boldly, while a harpsichordist gently tinkled. Bach's "Orchestral Suite No. 1" lacked rhythmic buoyancy, but Mr. Martins compensated with attention to dynamic contrast.

1. Choose the correct word.

> _____ song was a breath of fresh air in the otherwise dismal evening.
>
> There   They're   Their

2. What would you expect to find in *The Harvard Dictionary of Music*?

3. Edit the sentence.

> **sahkira is a artist for who I have grate admeeration.**

4. Complete the analogy.

> **calm : nervous :: melancholy : _____**

5. Write a proverb about music.

HE WHO PAYS THE PIPER CALLS THE TUNE.

MUSIC INDUCES MORE MADNESS THAN WINE.

MUSIC IS THE BEST CURE FOR A SORROWING MIND.

Read

Over There (1917)

introduced by Nora Bayes
words and music
George Michael Cohan, 1878-1942

Johnnie get your gun, get your gun, get your gun
Take it on the run, on the run, on the run
Hear them calling you and me
Ev'ry son of liberty
Hurry right away no delay go today
Make your daddy glad to have had such a lad
Tell your sweetheart not to pine
To be proud her boy's in line.

CHORUS:
Over there — over there —
Send the word, send the word over there
That the Yanks are coming the Yanks are coming
The drums rum-tum-ming ev'rywhere —
So prepare
We'll be over we're coming over
And we won't come back till it's over over there.

Johnnie get your gun, get your gun, get your gun
Johnnie show the Hun you're a son of a gun
Hoist the flag and let her fly
Yankee Doodle do or die
Pack your little kit show your grit do your bit
Yankees to the ranks from the towns and the tanks
Make your mother proud of you
And the old Red White and Blue.

When the *Lusitania* Went Down (1915)

by Charles McCarron and Nathaniel Vincent

The nation is sad as can be,
A message came over the sea,
A thousand more, who sailed from our shore,
Have gone to eternity.
The Statue of Liberty high
Must now have a tear in her eye,
I think, it's a shame,
Some one is to blame,
But all we can do is just sigh!

CHORUS:
Some of us lost a true sweet-heart,
Some of us lost a dear dad,
Some lost their mothers, sisters and brothers,
Some lost the best friends they had.
It's time they were stopping this warfare,
If women and children must drown,
Many brave hearts went to sleep in the deep,
When the *Lusitania* went down.

A lesson to all it should be,
When we feel like crossing the sea,
American ships, that sail from our slips,
Are safer for you and me.
A Yankee can go anywhere,
As long as Old Glory is there,
Altho' they were warned,
The warning they scorned,
And now must cry in despair.

1. Compare the **tone** and the **message** of the two World War I songs.
2. Compare the **tempo** of the two songs' lyrics. How do you think the rhythm of the words affects the tempo?
3. Relate this historical note to the lyrics of "When the *Lusitania* Went Down."

In February, 1915, the German government announced an unrestricted warfare campaign: Any ship taking goods to Allied countries was in danger of being attacked. The international agreements in force stated that commanders who suspected a non-military vessel of carrying war materials had to stop and search it, rather than do anything that would endanger the lives of the occupants. The sinking of the *Lusitania* by German boats had a profound impact on public opinion in the United States.

Write

Write song lyrics or a rap about an event that is important to you. Convey the way you feel about the event through the tone and tempo of the words.

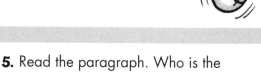

1. Edit the sentence.

   the home of the boston red sox is a ball park known as fenway?

2. The left field wall in Fenway Park is known as the Green Monster. The name is an example of what literary technique?

3. Choose the correct word.

   It is a (real, really) bad idea to eat so many hot dogs.

4. Many sports have specialized vocabulary. Explain the meaning of these words to a baseball player.

5. Read the paragraph. Who is the intended audience? What is the purpose of the "pitch"? Is the paragraph effective for the intended audience? for others?

Fenway—America's Most Beloved Park

Visit the park where the Babe pitched, The Kid hit, Yaz dazzled, and Manny and Ortiz still thrill young fans today. Soak up the rich history; hear the echoes of the past. Touch the Green Monster, imagine being one of the "Knights of the Keyboard" as you see the view from the Press Box; visit the State Street Pavilion Club before strolling around Fenway Park.

1. Add punctuation to clarify the meaning.

   Green and red lights on Fenways manual scoreboard signal balls strikes and outs

2. Which source would give you current statistics for Red Sox players?

   ○ StubHub.com—a site where fans buy tickets

   ○ redsox.mlb.com—the official Red Sox site

   ○ en.wikipedia.org—an online encyclopedia

3. Edit the sentence.

   a red seat in the right feild bleachers marks the spot where ted williams home run the longest measurable one hit in the park landed

4. Write a title for a news article about the fact that Fenway Park has not changed significantly since Opening Day in 1912.

5. Imagine an **unlikely** professional baseball player. Describe the character. (Your description should make it clear to the reader why the player is *unlikely*.)

Write: | **Draw a picture based on your description:**

1. Add commas to set off the appositive from the rest of the sentence.

> **Babe Ruth the famous homerun slugger was a Boston Red Sox player.**

2. Change these words to plural possessives.

> **base runner's cleats**
>
> **coach's signals**

3. Write an antonym for the word **triumph**.

4. Explain the metaphor.

> **The room behind the manual scoreboard, a three-dimensional autograph book, has signatures of famous players on its walls.**

5. If you were asked to guess in what decade the biggest crowd gathered at Fenway Park would you choose the 1930s or the 2000s? Read the passage below and tell whether you found the information surprising, and why or why not?

> The two biggest baseball crowds ever at Fenway Park were for a Yankees doubleheader on September 22, 1935 (47,627 fans), and a Detroit Tigers doubleheader on August 19, 1934 (46,995 fans). Those crowds will never be equaled under Fenway's current dimensions. Stringent fire laws and league rules prohibited the overcrowding that was so common in the 1930s. The current capacity of Fenway Park is 36,108.

1. Circle any correctly spelled words.

confuzion   decision

consipicuous   magicion

2. Rewrite the sentence with a plural subject.

> **The spirit of a legendary hero lingers in the Fenway Park dugout.**

3. What is an **index**?

4. Use the note to determine how much higher the Green Monster is than the center field wall and the right field fence.

> **The left field wall—the Green Monster—measures 37 feet high, with the screen above the wall extending 23 feet. The center field wall is 17 feet high, and the right field fence is 3 to 5 feet high.**

5. How did Fenway Park get its name?

_____Baseball Facts & Trivia

Boston Globe owner General Charles Henry Taylor, a Civil War veteran, bought the Red Sox for his son John I. Taylor in 1904. At various times the team was called the Puritans, the Pilgrims, and the Plymouth Rocks. In 1907, Taylor changed the club's name from the Pilgrims to the Red Sox. In 1910, he announced that he would build a ballpark for his Red Sox. Taylor dubbed the new ballpark Fenway Park because of its location in an area of Boston known as the Fens.

Read

Fenway Park • Boston, Massachusetts

Ticket Prices	
Loge Box	$85
Right Field Box	$45
Right Field Roof Box	$45
Infield Grandstand	$45
Outfield Grandstand	$27
Bleachers	$23
Upper Bleachers	$12
Standing Room	$20

PREMIUM SEATING

Field Box	$105
State Street Pavilion Club	$158
Home Plate Pavilion Club	$205
Dugout Box (Canvas Alley)	$130
Extended Dugout Box	$260
Dugout Box (Infield)	$312
EMC	$286
Pavilion Standing Room	$25
Green Monster	TBA
Right Field Roof Deck	TBA

Key

Future Game Ticket Sales	FG
Game Day Ticket Sales	GD
Game Day Will-Call Pickup	WC

1. What price would you pay for a seat in each of these sections?

upper bleachers_____   extended dugout box_____   right field roof box_____

2. Which section would you like to sit in and why?

3. Which sections should you avoid if you want to be able to read the message board without having to look behind you?

4. How much would outfield grandstand tickets cost for a family of six?

Write

Write concise directions to the Game Day Ticket Sales for someone arriving at Fenway Park.

_____
_____
_____
_____
_____
_____

1. Edit the sentence.

John Steinbecks mother a former school teacher fostered his love of reading and the written word.

2. How do you make an **inference**?

3. Explain Steinbeck's personification.

"Perfect live oaks grew in the meadow of the lovely place, and the hills hugged it jealously against the fog and the wind."

—Pastures of Heaven

4. Use the context to define **dissipated**.

"Gray smoke spurted up out of the stubby stovepipe, spurted up a long way before it spread out and dissipated."

—from *Breakfast* by John Steinbeck

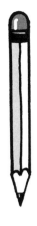

5. How did Steinbeck's experiences influence his writing?

- BORN IN SALINAS, CA (A SMALL TOWN IN A VALLEY OF LETTUCE FARMERS)
- PRESIDENT OF SENIOR CLASS IN HIGH SCHOOL
- WROTE FOR THE SCHOOL NEWSPAPER
- DROPPED OUT OF STANFORD UNIVERSITY
- JOBS – RANCH HAND, FACTORY WORKER, SALES CLERK, FREELANCE NEWSPAPER WRITER, CONSTRUCTION WORKER, FARM LABORER, WAR CORRESPONDENT

1. What is **compassion**?
How can an author show compassion?

2. Circle the explicit verbs.

His heavy horse scrambled and floundered up the steep slope; the manzanita reached sharp claws for the corporal's face, but he plunged after his dinner.

3. Add the commas.

John Steinbeck I think is an interesting man.

4. In 1962, when John Steinbeck won the Nobel Prize, he wrote, "This prize business is only different from the Lettuce Queen of Salinas in degree." Explain what you think he meant.

5. As Steinbeck wrote **East of Eden** he kept this record of ingredients:

RECIPE FOR WRITING SUCCESS

- eleven years of mental gestation
- one year of uninterrupted writing
- 25 dozen pencils
- approximately three dozen reams of paper
- 350,000 words (before editing)
- 75,000 words in a work-in-progress journal
- rock-hard callus on middle finger of right hand

Which ingredient do you think was most important and why?

WEDNESDAY WEEK 29

Name

LANGUAGE PRACTICE

1. Write a metaphor about ideas.

> **Ideas are like rabbits. You get a couple and learn how to handle them, and pretty soon you have a dozen.** —John Steinbeck

2. Choose the correct word.

> **I felt so (bad, badly) for Lennie that I cried.**

3. Edit the sentence.

> **Steinbeck persured his writting career in New York, but was unsucessful in geting published.**

4. In his Nobel Prize acceptance speech John Steinbeck said, "Literature is as old as speech. It grew out of human need for it and it has not changed except to become more needed." Do you agree that literature is more needed in this age of technology? Write a clear statement of your position and then list several ideas you could use to support the position.

5. In 1938, Steinbeck's *The Grapes of Wrath* brought nationwide attention to the living conditions and exploitation of farm workers. Steinbeck wrote:

"The vilification of me out here from the large landowners and bankers is pretty bad. I'm frightened at the rolling might of this damned thing. It is completely out of hand; I mean a kind of hysteria about the book is growing that is not healthy."

Think about a time *the rolling might of hysteria* influenced public opinion on another issue. What was the issue?

THURSDAY WEEK 29

Name

LANGUAGE PRACTICE

1. Choose the correct word.

> **The students were (afforded, eager) to get back to the novel.**

2. Edit the sentences.

> **during world war II steinbeck was a war correspondant for the new york herald tribune once there was a war published in 1958 is a collection of some of his dispatches**

3. What does a **coordinating conjunction** do?

4. Use editing marks to show proper punctuation and capitalization for the address.

> museum store
> the national steinbeck center
> one main street
> old town salinas ca 93901

5. Steinbeck toured America in a specially commissioned pickup truck he named Rocinante, after Quixote's horse.

Rocinante was not "mean" or "ugly-natured" like some cars. Indeed, because of her "purring motor and perfect performance," "because of her ready goodness," he treated her "like the honest bookkeeper, the faithful wife," and except for meticulous routine maintenance, he ignored her.

Write a description of your vehicle. Give the vehicle a personality. Is it mean-spirited or honest?

Read

The Wit and Wisdom of Steinbeck

a. "Man, unlike any other thing organic or inorganic in the universe, grows beyond his work, walks up in the stairs of his concepts, emerges ahead of his accomplishments."

(from **The Grapes of Wrath**)

d. "This I believe: That the free exploring mind of the individual is the most valuable thing in the world. And this I would fight for: the freedom of the mind to take any direction it wishes, undirected. And this I must fight against: any idea, religion, or government which limits or destroys the individual."

b. "I wonder why progress so often looks like destruction..."

(from **Travels With Charley**)

e. "So in our pride we ordered for breakfast an omelet, toast and coffee and what has just arrived is a tomato salad with onions, a dish of pickles, a big slice of watermelon, and two bottles of creme soda."

c. "The high gray-flannel fog of winter closed off the Salinas Valley from the sky and from all the rest of the world. On every side it sat like a lid on the mountains and made of the great valley a closed pot."

(from **The Chrysanthemums**)

f. "Where does discontent start? You are warm enough, but you shiver. You are fed, yet hunger gnaws at you. You have been loved, but your yearning wanders in new fields. And to prod all of these there's time, the Bastard Time.

A book is like a man—clever and dull, brave and cowardly, beautiful and ugly. For every flowering thought there will be a page like a wet and mangy mongrel, and for every looping flight a tap on the wing and a reminder that wax cannot hold the feathers firm too near the sun."

1. Choose b or c and explain the metaphor.
2. Paraphrase John Steinbeck's belief statement.
3. Give two examples of beginnings of discontent in your life. How are your examples influenced by time?
4. If pride did not dictate what you ordered for breakfast, what would you order?

Write

Think about Steinbeck's description of a book (f). Then write your own description of a book.

1. Explain the Chinese proverb.

> To understand your parents' love, you must raise children yourself.

2. What is an **ancestor**?

3. Edit the sentence.

> **At my family reunion I meet more relatives then I ever thought that I had.**

4. Write a sentence for each of the different meanings for the noun **family**.

   a. a group of people living together and functioning as a single household

   b. group of languages that have a common origin

   c. branch of the Mafia

   d. category in the taxonomic classification of related organisms

5. Record different types of families on this web. See how many you can think of.

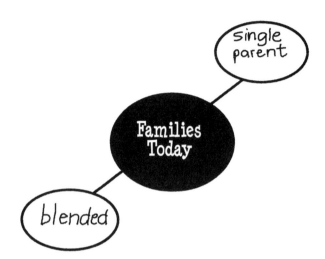

1. Use the context to define **nuclear family**.

> There are many types of families. The smallest family is that of two persons such as a husband and wife, a parent and child, or a brother and sister. These units are kinds of nuclear families. Nuclear families include any two or more persons related to one another by blood, marriage, or adoption who share a common residence.

2. Choose the correctly spelled words.

   ○ allowance   ○ allowence

   ○ neice   ○ niece

3. A research study found that the middle child of a family of three is usually different from the middle child of a large family. Use your experience to hypothesize several reasons this might be true.

4. What is a **bibliography**?

5. Humorist Erma Bombeck said:

> You hear a lot of dialogue on the death of the American family. Families aren't dying. They're merging into big conglomerates.

Explain what you think she meant.

1. Edit the sentence.

mom, susans mother is going to take us over to the mall and then her step-dad will bring both of us home

2. Explain what you think George Bernard Shaw meant when he said,

If you cannot get rid of the family skeleton, you may as well make it dance.

3. What is the meaning of **sibling**?

Sibling rivalry has existed as long as families.

4. Write a simile and an explanation that compares something in the kitchen to a family.

My family is like a stew pot. No matter what we put inside, we let it simmer and season it, and the result always tastes good.

5. The U.S. Census Bureau defines *family* in this way:

U.S Census Bureau ————————————
"A family includes a householder and one or more people living in the same household who are related by birth, marriage, or adoption. All people in a household who are related to the householder are regarded as members of his or her family."

What is your definition of family?

1. Edit the sentence.

Michael will finish the drivers ed class and then he can drive father to work.

2. Write a title for an article on a family with ten children, each of whom is a record-holding athlete.

3. What information would you need to know in order to answer the research question, "Do children from larger families have lower levels of education?"

4. Explain why this riddle is considered a pun.

What did the big Tomato say to his little tagalong brother?

Hey, Litl' Bro, Catsup!

puff

5. Summarize the information.

Frank J. Sulloway, a researcher at the Massachusetts Institute of Technology, studied the role of birth order in determining personality and social outlook. His research demonstrated that, because of the evolutionary hierarchy in families, first-born children are more likely to be conformists, while the later-borns tend to be more creative and more likely to reject the status quo. He suggested that a person tends to have more in common with any randomly chosen person of his or her own age than with a sibling.

Name

Read

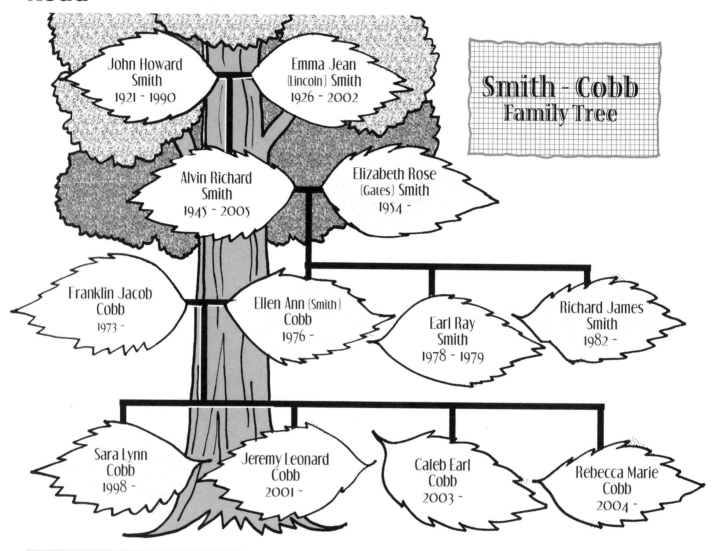

Smith - Cobb Family Tree

1. Explain the relationship between Richard James Smith and Caleb Earl Cobb.

2. Do Ellen and her husband Franklin believe in passing on family names (names handed down from one generation to another)?

3. What do you know about John Howard Smith and Earl Ray Smith?

Write

Create a family tree for your immediate family and at least two previous generations. Include a title and a caption for readers.

1. Give three synonyms for **ancient**.

2. What does this definition necessitate?

History is the written story of man.

3. What is an **artifact**?
Name three artifacts that future civilizations might use to characterize your civilization.

4. Edit the sentence.

Archaeologists have found evidence of primitive independent farming communities in the tigris and euphrates river valleys the nile river valley the indus valley and the huang he valley in china.

5. Write a short paragraph to summarize the information on the time line.

1509 – Michelangelo paints the ceiling of the Sistine Chapel.

1513 – Spanish explorer Ponce de Leon discovers Florida.

1517 – The Reformation begins as an attempt to reform the Roman Catholic Church, but results in a church split—leading to the formation of Protestant sects. Martin Luther, a Catholic monk, posts 95 theses on a church door, objecting to some practices and beliefs of the Catholic Church.

1519 – Portuguese explorer Ferdinand Magellan sets out on a journey to sail around the world. Natives in the Philippines kill him, but one of his ships completes the circumnavigation of the globe in 1522.

1. Edit the sentence.

one of the earlier civilizations grew up in an area that stretched from the eastern shores of the mediterranean sea between the tigris and euphrates rivers to the persian gulf

2. Do you agree? Tell why or why not.

Agriculture changed the lives of early nomadic peoples.

3. Use the context to define **cuneiform**.

The people of Sumer are credited with inventing the wheel as well as cuneiform, a form of writing.

4. Combine the two sentences for better flow.

A king of Assyria founded the first library.
It contained clay tablets with writing on many subjects.

5. Write a thesis sentence about literature in Mesopotamia.

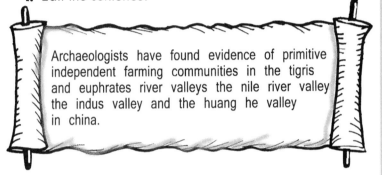

The finest literary work from ancient Mesopotamia is the *Epic of Gilgamesh*. Originally recited aloud, this towering work was probably recorded on clay tablets around 2000 B.C., more than one thousand years before the *Iliad* and the *Odyssey* were recorded in writing. *Gilgamesh* is a long narrative poem that describes the deeds of a hero in his quest for identity and the meaning of life. Part man and part god, Gilgamesh deals with such universal themes as the meaning of friendship, fear of sickness, death, and the forces of evil.

1. Circle the correctly spelled word.

acheivement   achievement

2. Edit the sentence.

a powerful babylonian king hammurabi create a set of laws hammurabi's code for his people.

3. Fact or opinion?

The Nile River provided transportation, food, and wood for the Egyptian people.

4. Use this portion of the outline to write about the ancient cities found in the Indus Valley.

A. Cities of the Indus Valley
1. large cities—Mohenjo-Daro, Harappa
2. well-organized
3. well-developed drainage and sewage
B. Tools and Crafts

5. Read the diagram and write a sentence comparing Athens and Sparta.

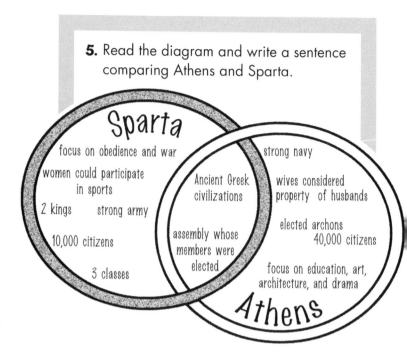

Sparta
focus on obedience and war
women could participate in sports
2 kings   strong army
10,000 citizens
3 classes

Ancient Greek civilizations
assembly whose members were elected

strong navy
wives considered property of husbands
elected archons
40,000 citizens
focus on education, art, architecture, and drama

Athens

1. Write a sentence about the contributions of this early African civilization.

Kush peoples
• **lived along the Nile River south of Egypt**
• **about 2000 B.C. to A.D. 350**
• **raised crops and cattle**
• **mined copper and gold**

2. What is the simple predicate?

The Hittites, as one of the first cultures to successfully smelt iron, were able to make stronger tools and weapons.

3. Edit the sentence.

Perhaps one might say that the ancient eyptians would be best remembered and appreciated for their magnificent pyramids.

4. What key words would you use to find facts about ancient Greek systems of government?

5. Compare the two structures.

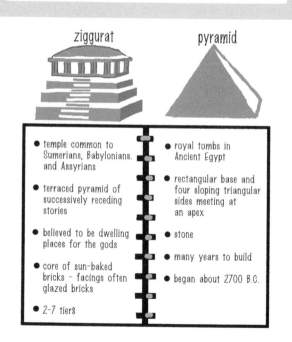

ziggurat   pyramid

• temple common to Sumerians, Babylonians. and Assyrians

• terraced pyramid of successively receding stories

• believed to be dwelling places for the gods

• core of sun-baked bricks - facings often glazed bricks

• 2-7 tiers

• royal tombs in Ancient Egypt

• rectangular base and four sloping triangular sides meeting at an apex

• stone

• many years to build

• began about 2700 B.C.

Looking for an Out-of-the-Ordinary Adventure?

Join us for a once-in-a-lifetime opportunity to travel back in time to witness the most magnificent creations of the ancient world. We'll spend one day at each of the Ancient Wonders of the World on this awe-inspiring seven-day Mediterranean foray.

We begin by setting the time machine dial at 600 B.C. and transporting back to the Hanging Gardens of Babylon. The King of Babylon's Gardens, located near the River Euphrates in modern day Iraq, feature a complex irrigation system. Come see for yourself if these mysterious Gardens really existed or were just an exaggerated description of Babylon's fertile landscape.

Our next stop takes us to Turkey, 50 years later, to the Temple of Artemis at Ephesus. We will admire the amazing marble facade and roam among the 120 60-foot columns. Together we'll appreciate this magnificent tribute to Artemis, the goddess of fertility, the wilderness, and wild animals.

On day three, we journey to 435 B.C. and the Greek town of Olympia to visit the cavernous temple that houses the glorious, dominating statue of Zeus. Zeus, the sky god and ruler of Mount Olympus, is seated in a massive throne at one end of the temple. Stand at Zeus' feet and gaze up, if you dare, to his head towering four stories above.

Next we return to Turkey in the year 350 B.C. Near the Aegean Sea, we will encounter the enchanting Mausoleum of Halicarnassus and admire its ornate statues. This structure was built as a burial chamber for King Mausollos, an otherwise ordinary leader who was immortalized in death. The origin of the word *mausoleum*, in fact, came from this remarkable structure.

Day five features another visit to Greece, this time to the island of Rhodes in 285 B.C. Here, astride the entrance to the island's harbor, we examine the 100-foot statue of the sun god Helios. Revel at the sight of the bronze Colossus of Rhodes glimmering in the Mediterranean sun above the bustling port.

Our final two stops take us to Egypt to see the oldest and youngest of the ancient wonders. On day six, we set our time machine to 220 B.C. and sail for the island of Pharos. Even from 30 miles away, we are able to appreciate the humongous Lighthouse at Alexandria. As we draw closer, you can see for yourself why this 40-story structure stood as an awesome symbol of Egypt's glory and an effective marker to warn ships of the dangerous conditions near the harbor.

To conclude our tour of the Ancient Wonders of the World, we go back in time more than four millennia to 2560 B.C. to find the Great Pyramid of Giza, built to house the sarcophagus of the Pharaoh Khufu. While we may never be able to imagine how this awe-inspiring behemoth was constructed with more than two million stones, we can appreciate its timeless design and the staggering manpower that must have gone into its creation. For our return journey, we'll turn the time gauge to modern day, but we'll remain in Giza. In this final magnificent twist, you'll see that the oldest wonder is also the only one still standing. As unbelievable as it seems, the beautiful Great Pyramid of Giza stands as tall and proud in the 21st Century as it did in 2560 B.C. Come see for yourself!

1. List the Seven Wonders of the World.

2. The brochure uses many synonyms for the word **trip**. Find four of them. Think of one more of your own.

3. Even though this piece is fiction it uses actual dates, locations, and factual descriptions. Is this approach a good way to present factual information? Why or why not?

Write

If you could travel on a time machine to any time and any place, where would you go and why?

Name

1. Explain the difference among these three newspaper articles.
- **news article**
- **feature articles**
- **editorials**

2. What is included in the dateline of a newspaper article?

3. George Bernard Shaw once said,

"**Newspapers are unable, seemingly, to discriminate between a bicycle accident and the collapse of civilization.**"

What do you think he meant?
Do you agree? Tell why or why not.

4. Explain a possible meaning of this headline. What literary device does it employ?

Fair Fare for Films

5. Edit the obituary.

 Chennai Times

Obituaries

chandralekha 78 an indian dancer and choreographer known for her philosophical fusing of the classical bharata natyam dance form with martial arts and therapeutic varieties of dance died on december 30 at her seaside home in the indian city of chennai

Name

1. Edit the sentence.

good conclusions to an editorial sums up arguements and spurs readers in to action

2. True or false?

If you can use the word *because* to show the relationship between events, the relation is causal, not just sequential.

3. Format a bibliography entry for an article in column three on page 27 in the *New York Times* of January 11, 2004. The article is entitled "Minute Tool Directs Enormous Drill in Search for Natural Gas".

4. Which argument is more effective and why?
- **a. Thousands of people thronged the concert.**
- **b. So many people attended the concert that the crowd formed the third largest city in the state.**

5. Rewrite the headlines to correct misconceptions.

Piccadilly Times
British Left Waffles on Falkland Islands

Barque Valley Bugle
Emergency Squad Helps Dog Bite Victim

Heartland Herald
Sisters Reunited After 18 Years at Checkout Counter

1. Think of five compound words that begin with the word **news**.

2. Sequence the installments of the cartoon strip.

___ Recovered Noxvillians Celebrate

___ Greater Noxville Stricken With Deadly Flu

___ Dr. Nox Discovers a Cure

3. Edit the sentence.

the line of words at the head of a newspaper story or article usualy printed in large type and giving the gist of the story or article that follows are the head line

4. True or false?

An effective editorial is direct, absorbing, and can move its readers to reevaluate an issue.

5. Write a metaphor that compares a newspaper to something in a classroom.

"More than print and ink, a newspaper is a collection of fierce individualists who somehow manage to perform the astounding daily miracle of merging their own personalities under the discipline of the deadline and retain the flavor of their own minds in print."

Arthur Ochs Sulzberger

1. Identify the underlined phrase.

<u>To write a newspaper column</u> is my secret ambition.

2. Write a headline for a newspaper article about the effects of record high temperatures during December in a ski resort area.

3. Explain what's wrong with these headlines:

a. **TERRORIST HEAD SEEKS ARMS**

b. **FARMER BILL DIES IN HOUSE**

4. Choose the correct word.

William Randolph Hearst wrote this (**advice, advise**) for would-be journalists.

"Try to be conspicuously accurate in everything, pictures as well as text. Truth is not only stranger than fiction, it is more interesting."

5. Donald M. Lowe, an educator and historian, observed:

"Newspapers have a different perceptual impact on the reader than the printed book. Unlike the linear development of a plot or an argument in the book, the concurrent reporting of news from different parts of the world make newspapers a mosaic of unrelated events."

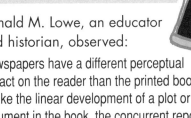

Make a list of some ways a newspaper and a book are different.

Read

Editorial Commentary

Dear Mr. Editor:

The *Leadville Post's* characterization of the proposed changes to Route 64 in the April 4 article "Botched Road Plan" was misleading and inaccurate. The *Post* failed to consult the main developer responsible for the changes, and the reporter, George Gray, clearly made no attempt to find out all the facts before writing his story. There were two glaring errors and one obvious omission in the article.

First, Mr. Gray mischaracterized the genesis of the plan by insinuating that the developer, Sun Construction, initiated discussions with the Leadville City Council. In fact, the City Council elicited proposals and a number of developers, including Sun Construction, responded. The *Post's* suggestion that Sun Construction went "fishing for business" is dishonest and erroneous.

The second error in Mr. Gray's article was to overstate the tax burden of the Route 64 development. The project will be entirely financed from existing road improvement funds and will not result in higher tax rates for the population of Leadville. By speculating about the costs, rather than confirming the facts with Sun Construction or the Leadville treasurer, Mr. Gray incites anger and resentment toward a project that will facilitate growth and support business development in eastern Leadville.

In addition to the errors above, Mr. Gray's "Botched Road Plan" also failed to mention a crucial component of the Route 64 planning process. *Post* readers would have benefited from the inclusion of the time, date, and location of the next Public Comment session on the Route 64 plan. The three previous sessions, in December, January, and March, were well attended, and feedback from public members shared during the sessions has been incorporated into the project development plan. Of course, including information about the Public Comment session would have run counter to Mr. Gray's shameless portrayal of Sun Construction as an overzealous, money-grubbing developer. Those *Post* readers who are interested in learning the truth behind the Route 64 project and sharing their own suggestions are invited to attend the Public Comment session on April 27, at 7 PM in the Elks Lodge on Main Street.

Thank you for the opportunity to clarify these facts and set the record straight about this crucial construction project. I hope Mr. Gray will be more diligent in his reporting on future capital projects.

Sincerely,

J. Little

CEO, Sun Construction

---

1. Although this letter was written to the *Leadville Post's* editor, who is the audience that J. Little hoped to reach and what is the purpose behind the article?

2. J. Little uses words with both negative and positive connotations to make his point in this editorial. List three words in each category.

3. What adjectives might J. Little use to describe Mr. Gray's investigative reporting?

4. Does this editorial make you question the validity of the "Botched Road Plan" article? Why?

Write

Think of a current-affair issue that you feel strongly about. Write a strong thesis sentence stating your opinion.

1. Circle the correct word.

The speed of the cars (surprise, surprises) us.

2. List three reasons for using natural gas as a fuel.

Natural gas is one of the cleanest burning alternative fuels available and offers a number of advantages over gasoline. Air exhaust emissions from natural gas vehicles are much lower than those from gasoline-powered vehicles. In addition, smog-producing gases, such as carbon monoxide and nitrogen oxides, and carbon dioxide are reduced significantly.

3. Yes or no?

The possessive of *it* is *it's*.

4. Explain the contradiction in the quotation.

The civilized man has built a coach, but has lost the use of his feet.
-*Ralph Waldo Emerson*

5. What qualifies a vehicle as an AFV?

Energy Policy Act
1992

Alternative-fuel vehicles, as defined by the Energy Policy Act of 1992, include any dedicated, flexible-fuel, or dual-fuel vehicles designed to operate on at least one alternative fuel. Alternative fuel vehicles come in a variety of vehicle models such as sedans, pickup trucks, sport utility vehicles, vans, shuttle buses, medium-duty vehicles (such as delivery trucks), heavy-duty buses, and heavy-duty trucks.

1. Give two synonyms for **acceleration**.

2. Add dashes to emphasize the comment.

The sleek new car the first she ever owned was her most prized possession.

3. Paraphrase the text to explain one of the problems in evaluating alternative fuels.

There are different benefits, trade-offs, and considerations when it comes to alternative fuels. It is difficult to compare "apples to apples" because benefits depend on the vehicles that use the fuel.

4. New models of automobiles are often named for animals. Think of a new model. List the attributes of the vehicle. Then give it an appropriate animal name.

COUGAR   MUSTANG   _____

5. Explain in easy-to-understand language the alternative fuel *ethanol*.

Ethanol (ethyl alcohol, grain alcohol, EtOH) is a clear, colorless liquid. Ethanol (CH_3CH_2OH) is made up of a group of chemical compounds whose molecules contain a hydroxyl group, $-OH$, bonded to a carbon atom. The Clean Air Act Amendments of 1990 mandated the sale of oxygenated fuels in areas with unhealthy levels of carbon monoxide. In the United States each year, approximately two billion gallons are added to gasoline to increase octane and improve the emissions quality of gasoline.

1. Evaluate the names of these hybrid electric vehicles. Choose the one name you find most appealing. Explain why you think it is appropriate for an AFV.

Green Line *Escape* PRIUS *Sierra*

2. Is this sentence a benefit or a disadvantage?

In actual use, drivers using ethanol can expect a fuel economy reduction of at least 15% relative to gasoline.

3. Write an antonym for **efficiency**.

4. What topic might be addressed in this article?

Advances in Car Technology Bring High-class Headaches

5. Read the notes. Write a thesis sentence about using fuel cells as a source of fuel for vehicles.

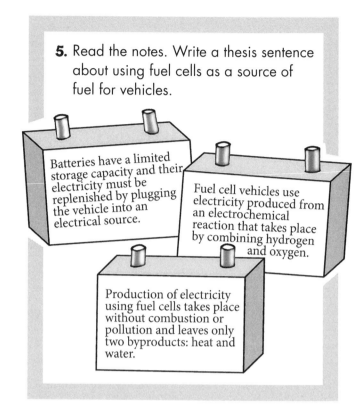

Batteries have a limited storage capacity and their electricity must be replenished by plugging the vehicle into an electrical source.

Fuel cell vehicles use electricity produced from an electrochemical reaction that takes place by combining hydrogen and oxygen.

Production of electricity using fuel cells takes place without combustion or pollution and leaves only two byproducts: heat and water.

1. Edit where necessary.

car and driver magazine
how to buy a new car by jeff holden
kelley blue book

2. Punctuate the sentence correctly.

Thanks to the latest electronics cars can tell you the pressure in each tire display stock quotes or give directions to the nearest Italian restaurant.

3. List three adjectives that you would use to describe a fast sportscar.

4. The Alternative Fuels Data Center (AFDC) is an online collection of data, including more than 3,000 documents and several interactive tools. The site is sponsored by the U.S. Department of Energy. Would you consider the site an unbiased source for research? Why or why not?

Driver's Manual

5. After reading this explanation would you continue to research hydrogen-powered vehicles as a positive alternative to traditionally powered vehicles? Why? What words influenced your opinion?

Although they are still in development, hydrogen vehicles represent an attractive option for reducing petroleum consumption and improving air quality.

Read

WELCOME TO THE NATIONAL AUTO SHOW, 2025!

Feast your eyes on the holographic marvel before you. It's the latest, greatest addition to the Futurific line of vehicles: The Flexor.

THIS IS NOT YOUR GRANDMOTHER'S HYBRID!

FLEXOR

The lustrous machine you see before you is completely powered by the rays of the sun. The powerful solar panels are hidden in tiny microchips located between the posterior racing fins and on top of the fully gyrating side mirrors. All six wheels are made of a resilient, self-repairing rubber-titanium compound that can handle any surface from mud to concrete, freezing ice to scorching sand.

You can enjoy Flexor's highly responsive steering and braking capabilities, or sit back and relax as the autopilot does the driving. The onboard, interactive computer system can be programmed to independently reach a particular destination or operate in "partner mode", acting as a second set of eyes and ears in emergency situations.

In the extremely improbable event of an accident, the Flexor is equipped with the patented Futuristic SafetySurround Bubble. If the on-board computer senses a foreign object, a tree, a tractor trailer, or even a deer, the SafetySurround Bubble will inflate and momentarily levitate the Flexor to a height of 15 feet above the ground. You will be safely out of harm's way, looking down from your luxurious leather seat, thanks to the most sophisticated vehicular shield on the market today!

CAN'T LOOK AWAY? DON'T DELAY. BUY TODAY! THE FLEXOR IS HERE TO STAY.

1. Explain the phrase, "This is not your grandmother's hybrid."

2. What important attributes does the exhibitor point out?

3. How does the Flexor differ from automobiles on the market today?

4. What do you think the Flexor looks like? Describe it in words or as an illustration.

Write

Write a note from a new teenage driver to a parent asking for a new car.

1. **Endemic** and **epidemic** share a common suffix. Do the two words have similar meanings?

2. Edit the sentence.

   tamaras absense was the result of a bad case of neumonia

3. If you are sick should you take an **anecdote**? Explain.

4. Summarize the entry. Is bruxism contagious? life-threatening? caused by a virus? diagnosable?

   Bruxism is the term for grinding your teeth or clenching your jaw. It occurs most often while a person is asleep. The American Dental Association says that the most common cause is stress, but other factors include sleep disorders, poor jaw or bite alignment, and poor tooth alignment. Symptoms of bruxism include headaches, jaw pain, and painful, loose teeth.

5. Read the graph. What does this graph show? What conclusions might you draw after reading it?

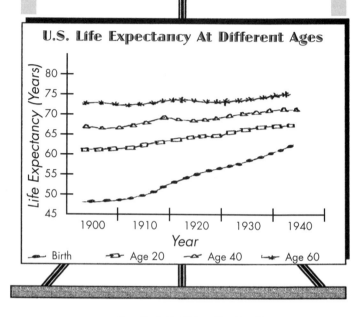

1. Label these words to indicate a negative, positive, or neutral connotation.

   ___ unwell   ___ under the weather
   ___ poorly   ___ unwholesome
   ___ ailing   ___ incapacitated
   ___ laid up   ___ pale
   ___ diseased   ___ peaked

2. Circle any correctly spelled words.

   absense   symptom

   disaese   physisian

3. W. C. Fields once said, "The best cure for insomnia is to get a lot of sleep." Why is this a humorous line?

4. List as many "aches" as you can that are compound words.

OSTEOPOROSIS

know the facts

• gender—osteoporosis more likely in women

• age— longer one lives, greater the chance

• family history— runs in families

• body size— small bones and thin build increase risk

• ethnicity—white and Asian women at higher risk

• diet—calcium and vitamin D help build strong bones

• physical activity—exercise keeps bones strong

• smoking—lowers estrogen level, boosts risk

5. What can you conclude about the risk factors for osteoporosis? Is it possible to change some of them?

1. Write a sentence that shows you understand the different meanings given for the word **sick**.

   a. noun, people who are not well

   b. adjective, queasy

   c. adjective, disgusting

2. Name one cause and one effect of a headache.

3. Complete the analogy.

   penicillin : antibiotic : : _____ : _____

4. If a disease is **contagious**, what does that mean? Can you think of something besides a disease that might be contagious?

   Boredom is contagious.
   Snore!

5. Author Eleanor Coerr wrote a true story about a Japanese girl. The tagline on the cover of the book reads:

MEET SADAKO

The star of her school's running team, Sadako is lively and athletic... until the dizzy spells start.

Explain how this sentence is an example of **foreshadowing**.

1. What are the implications of the World Health Organization's definition of **health**?

   Health is a state of complete physical, mental and social well-being, and not merely the absence of disease or infirmity.

2. Edit the sentence.

   All infants should recieve the first dose of hepatitis b vaccine soon after he is born and before he is discharged from the hospitel.

3. Give the comparative and superlative forms of **ill**.

4. Write three adjectives that could be used to describe a character who looks:

   • **healthy**

   • **unhealthy**

5. Explain how an antihistamine works. Relate your explanation to the meaning of the prefix **anti-**.

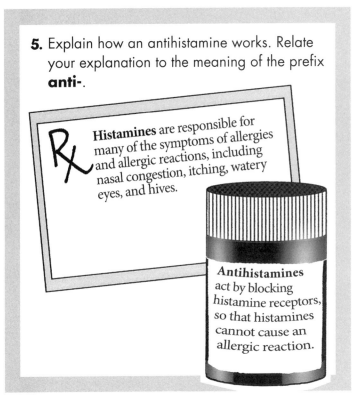

R **Histamines** are responsible for many of the symptoms of allergies and allergic reactions, including nasal congestion, itching, watery eyes, and hives.

Antihistamines act by blocking histamine receptors, so that histamines cannot cause an allergic reaction.

Read

For generations, getting the chicken pox was an itchy, scratchy rite of passage. At some point before their fifteenth birthdays, most children would endure five to ten days of a blistery rash, fever, cough, and exhaustion. Suffering from chicken pox would normally only occur once, because the body developed immunity after the first case. But since a vaccine became available in 1995, fewer and fewer children in the United States are facing the oatmeal baths and calamine lotion applications that were used for years to treat the bumpy red spots caused by the varicella-zoster virus (VZV).

Many states now require the chicken pox vaccine for children attending public schools. Chicken pox is extremely contagious and, prior to widespread vaccination efforts, entire classes, sports teams, or families would sometimes be infected at the same time. School absences and medical costs associated with the chicken pox virus have declined significantly since the introduction of the vaccine.

Despite the vaccine's success, there are still serious cases and even deaths from chicken pox each year. Complications are most likely to occur in unvaccinated adults who never contracted chicken pox during childhood and vulnerable populations such as infants or persons with weakened immune systems. In rare instances, even those who have been vaccinated can get the chicken pox, but these cases are normally very mild.

1. Use the context to define the phrase **rite of passage**.

2. What details explain why states require the chicken pox vaccine be given to children attending public schools?

3. What is the purpose of this article and what audience will probably read it?

4. True or false?

   Serious cases of chicken pox are a thing of the past.

Write

Write a concluding sentence for the informational article on chicken pox. You might begin with this sentence starter:

   Thanks to the chicken pox vaccine, . . .

1. Here is one definition of language.

Language is a system, used for communication—a set of arbitrary symbols that can be combined productively to convey new information.

Name at least one additional attribute that should be included in the definition.

2. Write six words that have the prefix tele-. Give a definition for each.

3. Cite rules for using **can** and **may**.

4. What is literal language? What is its opposite?

5. Identify the tone in this excerpt from an article "What Is Communication?" by Liza Nova.

The Communication Digest_____

continued from page 37
...The evening news anchors drone on from their TV soapboxes, reading a script and sometimes faltering, and the masses are being communicated to. An office cubicle dweller receives an email from the manager who sits two desks away, and there's communication going on there...

1. Epictetus, the Greek philosopher, advised:

"We have two ears and one mouth so that we can listen twice as much as we speak."

Write your own piece of advice for effective communication.

2. Edit the sentence. Reorder the phrases if you think it will help the flow of the sentence.

A pioneer in the field of telecommunications alexander graham bell was born in 1847 in edinburgh scotland

3. Explain the origin of the word **telephone**.

4. Circle the complete subject.

Advances are constantly being made in the field of cell phone technology, which means that there are always newer cell phone models coming out on the market.

5. Edit the quotation.

for centuries humans have tried to teach animals to communicate like humans said Michael Darre, an animal science professor at the university of connecticut and now we're getting to the point where we're saying wait a second why don't we learn their language instead of making them learn ours

1. Edit the sentence.

> just as the vacume tube and the transister made possible the early telephone network the wireless revolution began only after low cost micro processors miniture circiut boreds and digital switching became available

2. True or false?

> An exclamation point or question mark is placed inside quotation marks when it punctuates the quotation.

3. List three alternatives to "Hello!".

4. Peter Drucker recognized a communication truth when he said, "The most important thing in communication is to hear what isn't being said." Reflect on how this quotation carries implications for developing characters in your writing.

5. Circle the words that are examples of onomatopoeia.

Elephants communicate with one another in a number of ways, including sound, sight, touch, and scent. But it is the noises they make– a repertoire of rumbles, roars, trumpets, bellows, cries, screams, and snorts that span almost ten octaves, including sounds that humans cannot hear– that scientists find the most challenging to comprehend.

-National Geographic

Write some other onomatopoetic words.

1. Anne Morrow Lindbergh observed, "Good communication is as stimulating as black coffee, and just as hard to sleep after." Write your own simile about communication.

2. List eight explicit verbs that could be used instead of the verb **said**.

3. Write two antonyms for communication.

4. Define the words **plan**, **anytime**, and **cell** as used in the advertisement. About how much per minute does the 900 Anytime Minutes plan cost?

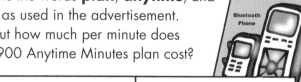

Motorola v3
Blue RAZAR

Bluetooth
Phone

FREE CELL PHONE	450 Anytime Minutes $39.99
Regular Price - $399.99 Your Price - $ 0.00	900 Anytime Minutes $59.99
$20 mail-in rebate with new Cingular service plan	1350 Anytime Minutes $79.99

5. List three advantages of **Carhood** and three disadvantages.

Norwegian Designer Lieke Ypma has an idea to enhance communication while driving and make it safer—**Carhood**. Aiming to engender a neighborhood spirit among drivers, as opposed to the kill-or-be-killed gladiator mentality out there today, Carhood enables a wireless LAN connection with a 300-meter range. Rather than fume silently, drivers can conduct a social roundtable as they sit in gridlock. To communicate with another Carhood-equipped vehicle, simply call them using a roof-mounted module. The driver of the other car completes the connection and a conversation is initiated, like a complicated version of the CB radio.

Read

The West Valley Viewpoint

Cell Phones Integral to Students' Lives

Cell phones are an integral part of students' lives and should not be banned from schools. Students need to have access to their phones throughout the school day and should not be expected to leave their phones in their lockers or cars, or, even worse, at home. While cell phones should not be used during class, students must be able to have their cell phones with them in case they need to access their schedules, look up a phone number or address, or make an emergency call. Many students use their cell phones to communicate with their parents during school hours, sharing changes in afterschool plans, passing on information about grades, or confirming pick-up times. Banning cell phones from schools is essentially forbidding student-parent communication during school hours. It is time to move into the 21st century and accept cell phones as a customary and essential part of students' lives.

Cell Phones Disruptive

Cell phones should be banned from schools because they are disruptive, unnecessary, and potentially unfair. Students cannot concentrate on learning if ringing and beeping cell phones constantly interrupt them. Cell phones are also disruptive to teachers, particularly if students are playing games or sending text messages during class. There is no need for students to have cell phones during school hours. If parents need to contact their children during the school day, the school administrative office can facilitate the communication. Most issues can wait until after school hours, and the truly urgent ones, which are rare, can be passed on to the student as required. In addition to being distracting to the learning environment and unnecessary, cell phones could also be used to cheat during class. The advanced features of many phones, such as camera and photo storage capabilities, make collecting and sharing information extremely easy. Students could bring answers with them to tests or share answers with other students during class using cell phones undetected by teachers. Cell phones are undermining education and have no place in the classroom.

1. Make a simple t-chart that shows the arguments for and against cell phone use at school.

2. The word **disruptive** has many synonyms. Rank each word on the following list from least negative (1) to most negative (6) in its connotations.

   ____ bothersome

   ____ inconvenient

   ____ distracting

   ____ niggling

   ____ troublesome

   ____ riotous

3. Explain this statement.

   Both arguments "color" the facts by using emotionally charged statements.

Write

Do you think cell phones should be banned from schools? Design a button that states your position.

1. Cross out the words that are unnecessary.

Imagining the envisioned evening ahead the pair of two flushed friends glowed with expected anticipation.

2. If a character shows **pathos** would he be a good friend?

3. Cantus Fraggle, the Muppet character, gave this advice. Expound on the simple statement to relate it to an incident where listening was important in your world.

Listening is the first step and the last step.

4. Write at least six synonyms for **friend**.

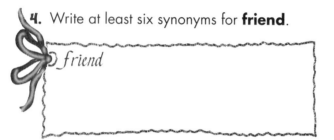

friend

5. In Truman Capote's **A Christmas Memory** a young boy describes his unlikely best friend, an elderly cousin.

A woman with shorn white hair is standing at the kitchen window. She is wearing tennis shoes and a shapeless gray sweater over a summer calico dress. She is small and sprightly, like a bantam hen; but, due to a long youthful illness, her shoulders are pitifully hunched. . . . "Oh my," she exclaims, her breath smoking the windowpane, "it's fruitcake weather!" The person to whom she is speaking is myself. I am seven; she is sixty-something . . . We are each other's best friend.

Analyze Capote's description: What does he reveal about the character without saying it directly?

1. Edit the sentence.

Mark Twain said good friends good books and a sleepy conscience this is the ideal life

2. Write a good title for an article about the experiences of friends at a boarding school.

3. Correct the spelling.

a. hopeing

b. choise

c. safty

4. Jim Henson, creator of the Muppets, said, "I believe that we can use television and film to be an influence for good." Do you agree? State your position and support it.

5. Sometimes friendship exists between a character and an inanimate object. Children often have "friends" that are stuffed animals or blankets. Others see books, trees, or music as friends. Think of a thing in your life which has the attributes of a friend. Write an ode to the object.

AN ODE TO MY BEAR . . .

1. What is the meaning of the underlined word?

We become <u>just</u> by performing just action . . . .
—*Aristotle*

2. Circle the infinitives. Tell how each is used.

To be a friend is to listen sympathetically to whining and to respond with sound judgment.

3. Complete the analogy.

frenetic : friend :: _____ : gravel

4. Edit the entry in the autograph book.

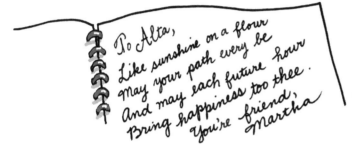

To Alta,
Like sunshine on a flour
may your path every be
And may each future hour
Bring happiness too thee.
You're friend,
Martha

5. Friends share sorrows as well as joys. Countee Cullen uses similes to describe this exchange. Identify the simile in this excerpt. Then paraphrase the message in this stanza.

Your grief and mine
Must intertwine
Like sea and river,
Be fused and mingle,
Diverse yet single,
Forever and forever.

– from "Any Human to Another"

1. Write the plural form of each word.

buddy   acquaintance   ally   pal

2. What is **hypocrisy**?

3. Correct the misspelled words.

innacent   curteous   sympathatec

4. In "From the Hymn of Empedocles" Matthew Arnold uses a question to make a statement about the importance of friendship. What is he saying?

Is it so small a thing

To have enjoy'd the sun,

To have lived light in the spring,

To have loved, to have thought, to have done;

To have advanced true friends,
    and beat down
    baffling foes;

5. What does the kite represent in this passage?

A stooped figure, a barren field, a palsied hand hoists a bright yellow rectangle high . . . A wind burst, a gentle pull, and the kite lifts and sails gracefully . . . The wrinkled face is lit by a young smile. One tear runs down the weathered cheek.

Name

Read

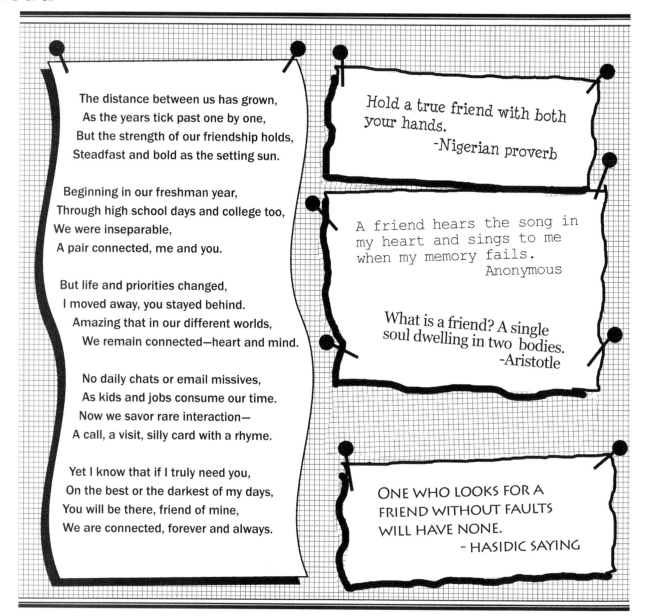

The distance between us has grown,
As the years tick past one by one,
But the strength of our friendship holds,
Steadfast and bold as the setting sun.

Beginning in our freshman year,
Through high school days and college too,
We were inseparable,
A pair connected, me and you.

But life and priorities changed,
I moved away, you stayed behind.
Amazing that in our different worlds,
We remain connected—heart and mind.

No daily chats or email missives,
As kids and jobs consume our time.
Now we savor rare interaction—
A call, a visit, silly card with a rhyme.

Yet I know that if I truly need you,
On the best or the darkest of my days,
You will be there, friend of mine,
We are connected, forever and always.

Hold a true friend with both your hands.
-Nigerian proverb

A friend hears the song in my heart and sings to me when my memory fails.
Anonymous

What is a friend? A single soul dwelling in two bodies.
-Aristotle

ONE WHO LOOKS FOR A FRIEND WITHOUT FAULTS WILL HAVE NONE.
- HASIDIC SAYING

1. The first poet uses the term "connected" repetitively.
   a. Define *connected* as it is used.
   b. From your experience, give an example of a positive connection and a negative connection.
2. Compare any two of the notes about friendship.
3. What color is friendship? Give reasons for your answer.
4. What does friendship sound like?

Write

Write a proverb about friendship. Try to express a big idea in a few words.

INCENTIVE PUBLICATIONS DAILY PRACTICE SERIES
GRADE 9 LANGUAGE SKILLS

Vocabulary & Word Skills

Skill	1	2	3	4	5	6	7	8	9	10	11	12	13	14	15	16	17	18	19	20	21	22	23	24	25	26	27	28	29	30	31	32	33	34	35	36
Knowledge of word meanings	✓	✓	✓	✓	✓	✓	✓	✓	✓	✓	✓	✓	✓	✓	✓	✓	✓	✓	✓	✓	✓	✓	✓	✓	✓	✓	✓		✓	✓	✓	✓	✓	✓	✓	✓
Word and phrase meaning from context	✓	✓	✓	✓	✓	✓	✓	✓	✓	✓	✓	✓	✓	✓	✓	✓	✓	✓	✓	✓	✓	✓	✓	✓	✓	✓	✓	✓	✓	✓	✓	✓	✓	✓	✓	✓
Denotation and connotation	✓	✓	✓			✓	✓	✓							✓																					
Identify synonyms	✓				✓					✓			✓		✓			✓								✓					✓		✓		✓	
Identify antonyms		✓											✓		✓											✓						✓				
Words with similar meanings or sounds	✓	✓				✓	✓			✓						✓			✓						✓	✓	✓			✓						
Homonyms, homophones, & homographs	✓	✓					✓		✓					✓		✓					✓	✓	✓			✓				✓					✓	
Multiple meaning words	✓				✓		✓			✓		✓	✓								✓	✓				✓		✓								
Analogies									✓	✓										✓	✓				✓									✓		✓
Prefixes, suffixes, and roots	✓		✓	✓			✓								✓								✓	✓	✓									✓		
Word origins and derivations	✓					✓										✓									✓		✓									✓

Reading Comprehension Skills

Skill	1	2	3	4	5	6	7	8	9	10	11	12	13	14	15	16	17	18	19	20	21	22	23	24	25	26	27	28	29	30	31	32	33	34	35	36
Main ideas		✓		✓	✓				✓	✓	✓	✓	✓	✓					✓	✓	✓	✓	✓		✓				✓	✓	✓		✓	✓		✓
Supporting details		✓		✓	✓	✓				✓		✓				✓					✓		✓													
Sequence		✓													✓				✓		✓		✓										✓		✓	
Expository—Identify, read, and comprehend expository selections				✓	✓				✓								✓		✓				✓			✓		✓	✓				✓			
Find information		✓		✓	✓				✓	✓				✓			✓						✓							✓						
Narrative	✓																	✓																		
Cause and Effect																																		✓		
Interpret graphs, tables, illustrations, graphics	✓			✓												✓							✓			✓			✓							
Classify opinions and facts											✓				✓	✓				✓												✓				✓
Argumentative—Identify strategies									✓						✓	✓						✓														
Draw conclusions		✓	✓	✓			✓						✓			✓	✓		✓		✓		✓		✓	✓		✓	✓	✓						
Make inferences		✓	✓			✓	✓		✓				✓				✓		✓		✓		✓			✓				✓						
Make predictions																										✓		✓								
Compare and contrast							✓									✓						✓		✓	✓					✓		✓				
Summarize		✓						✓			✓			✓					✓				✓	✓										✓		✓
Evaluate		✓		✓				✓							✓	✓			✓			✓	✓	✓					✓			✓		✓		
Persuasive							✓											✓															✓			
Paraphrase text	✓		✓					✓						✓			✓					✓			✓			✓		✓					✓	
Make & support generalizations from reading	✓								✓																	✓					✓			✓		

Usage Skills

Skill	1	2	3	4	5	6	7	8	9	10	11	12	13	14	15	16	17	18	19	20	21	22	23	24	25	26	27	28	29	30	31	32	33	34	35	36
Subject/verb agreement			✓		✓				✓		✓	✓			✓	✓	✓		✓		✓	✓	✓	✓	✓	✓			✓	✓	✓	✓	✓	✓		✓
Use singular and plural nouns correctly							✓		✓														✓			✓	✓	✓						✓		
Proper word choice: who or whom; affect or effect; can or may; real or really; accept or except, etc.	✓					✓		✓			✓					✓									✓		✓				✓					

113

Use It! Don't Lose It! IP 612-4

© 2007 Incentive Publications, Inc., Nashville, TN

INCENTIVE PUBLICATIONS DAILY PRACTICE SERIES
GRADE 9 LANGUAGE SKILLS

Literature Skills

Skill	1	2	3	4	5	6	7	8	9	10	11	12	13	14	15	16	17	18	19	20	21	22	23	24	25	26	27	28	29	30	31	32	33	34	35	36
Identify and analyze setting, plot, characters, theme, tone, mood, point of view	√																										√								√	
Classify writing genres and modes					√			√		√				√	√					√				√	√								√			√
Identify literary devices: simile, metaphor, alliteration, puns, rhyme, rhythm, idioms, onomatopoeia, personification, hyperbole, imagery, repetition, oxymoron, paradox, cliché, allusion, irony, dialect and jargon, dialogue, sensory language, flashbacks, foreshadowing, language structure, colloquial language, and symbolism	√		√				√				√			√	√				√	√	√	√		√		√	√	√	√		√		√	√	√	√
Identify author's audience and purpose		√		√				√	√			√																√					√	√		
Identify different types of poetry: haiku, sonnet, quatrain, epic, ballad, blank verse; and elements of plays																√							√				√					√				
Identify an author's use of persuasion, bias, and propaganda									√							√						√		√												
Relate literary works to their historical context and culture																					√	√	√													
Analyze an author's style			√		√			√		√			√					√			√								√						√	√
Analyze characterization	√							√									√																	√		√
Identify characteristics of different genre and modes			√															√								√			√						√	√
Compare ways authors organize, present ideas					√					√		√						√	√		√			√	√		√		√		√	√	√		√	√
Analyze an author's word choice		√	√		√			√		√	√	√		√	√	√		√	√	√	√	√	√	√	√	√	√	√	√	√	√	√	√	√	√	√
Make connections with personal experiences			√	√	√		√						√																							

Grammar Skills

Skill	1	2	3	4	5	6	7	8	9	10	11	12	13	14	15	16	17	18	19	20	21	22	23	24	25	26	27	28	29	30	31	32	33	34	35	36
Parts of Speech	√				√		√	√	√		√	√	√	√			√	√	√			√		√	√	√	√	√	√		√	√				√
Pronouns: relative, indefinite, interrogative		√					√				√					√			√																	√
Verbs	√				√		√	√			√	√	√	√	√		√				√		√		√				√			√		√		
Subjects and predicates			√				√		√	√					√					√						√			√							
Direct and indirect objects		√					√					√			√																					
Possessive nouns	√						√							√				√	√			√					√						√			
Phrases: prepositional, appositive, and verbal—participle, gerund, and infinitive	√					√																		√				√	√			√				√
Different kinds of clauses: independent, subordinate, adjective, adverb, noun, essential, and nonessential									√											√		√							√							
Verb tenses		√														√								√	√			√		√						
Pronoun case: nominative, objective, possessive		√		√		√											√			√	√		√		√	√	√					√	√			
Subject/verb, subject/pronoun agreement			√		√			√								√							√	√		√					√		√	√		√
Degrees of comparison: positive, comparative, and superlative			√	√																														√		
Misplaced modifiers				√									√					√	√					√										√		

Spelling Skill

Skill	1	2	3	4	5	6	7	8	9	10	11	12	13	14	15	16	17	18	19	20	21	22	23	24	25	26	27	28	29	30	31	32	33	34	35	36
Spell words correctly	√	√	√	√	√	√	√	√	√	√	√	√	√	√	√	√	√	√	√	√	√	√	√	√	√	√	√	√	√	√	√	√	√	√	√	√

Use It! Don't Lose It! IP 612-4

INCENTIVE PUBLICATIONS DAILY PRACTICE SERIES
GRADE 9 LANGUAGE SKILLS

Writing Skills

Skill	1	2	3	4	5	6	7	8	9	10	11	12	13	14	15	16	17	18	19	20	21	22	23	24	25	26	27	28	29	30	31	32	33	34	35	36
Use graphic organizers to organize information and take notes																																				
Descriptive writing				✓	✓	✓		✓	✓		✓				✓	✓	✓	✓	✓	✓			✓			✓		✓	✓			✓	✓	✓	✓	
Write in different genres and modes	✓							✓	✓			✓				✓	✓	✓	✓	✓	✓	✓			✓	✓			✓	✓		✓	✓		✓	
Write topic sentences							✓				✓	✓				✓	✓							✓					✓			✓				
Add supporting details					✓				✓		✓	✓				✓	✓		✓			✓	✓						✓			✓	✓		✓	
Use explicit verbs		✓										✓																						✓		
Write captions and titles						✓	✓			✓					✓				✓									✓							✓	
Identify sentence fragments, run-on sentences										✓				✓							✓													✓		
Write strong beginnings, endings, thesis stmts.			✓										✓				✓	✓			✓						✓		✓		✓			✓		
Summarize a written piece or information						✓								✓					✓	✓				✓	✓			✓	✓			✓				
Paraphrase sentences or writings														✓										✓												
Respond to a written piece or thesis statement					✓		✓	✓							✓										✓											
Proofread and use proofreading symbols for spelling, usage, punctuation, capitalization	✓			✓					✓		✓		✓					✓	✓	✓	✓					✓	✓						✓		✓	
Revise for clarity, word choice, effectiveness, sequence, flow			✓	✓		✓					✓		✓									✓					✓		✓				✓			
Support a premise	✓		✓								✓										✓				✓										✓	
Combine short sentences for readability		✓		✓		✓		✓			✓					✓		✓					✓						✓							✓

Capitalization & Punctuation Skills

Skill	1	2	3	4	5	6	7	8	9	10	11	12	13	14	15	16	17	18	19	20	21	22	23	24	25	26	27	28	29	30	31	32	33	34	35	36
Capitalization of proper nouns and adjectives	✓	✓	✓	✓	✓	✓		✓	✓	✓	✓	✓					✓	✓	✓	✓	✓	✓			✓	✓	✓	✓	✓	✓	✓	✓	✓		✓	✓
Capitalizations of titles	✓	✓				✓	✓		✓		✓		✓		✓		✓	✓		✓	✓					✓	✓		✓			✓				
Capitalizing words in sentences	✓	✓	✓	✓	✓	✓	✓	✓	✓		✓		✓		✓		✓	✓	✓	✓	✓	✓	✓	✓	✓	✓	✓	✓	✓	✓	✓	✓	✓	✓	✓	✓
End punctuation	✓	✓			✓	✓	✓	✓					✓	✓			✓			✓					✓				✓					✓	✓	
Commas	✓		✓	✓	✓	✓	✓	✓	✓	✓		✓	✓	✓				✓		✓		✓	✓	✓	✓		✓	✓	✓	✓			✓	✓	✓	
Quotation Marks									✓										✓	✓	✓					✓					✓					✓
Parentheses, dashes, and hyphens			✓	✓									✓			✓			✓						✓	✓		✓								
Apostrophes	✓					✓		✓	✓			✓		✓		✓			✓		✓				✓		✓				✓					
Capitalization and punctuation in quotations		✓		✓			✓		✓						✓		✓				✓		✓	✓												✓

Study & Research Skills

Skill	1	2	3	4	5	6	7	8	9	10	11	12	13	14	15	16	17	18	19	20	21	22	23	24	25	26	27	28	29	30	31	32	33	34	35	36
Outlines							✓							✓								✓								✓			✓	✓		
Purposes and uses of different reference materials and reading strategies	✓				✓			✓			✓				✓				✓					✓			✓				✓					
Using reference works: almanacs, atlases, dictionaries, encyclopedia entries, maps, charts, graphs, card catalogs	✓		✓							✓			✓					✓		✓		✓	✓		✓			✓	✓					✓	✓	
Document sources using appropriate citation format																	✓	✓	✓				✓	✓			✓				✓					
Evaluate quality, usefulness of reference mtrls.				✓		✓						✓			✓					✓			✓		✓	✓		✓			✓	✓				
Identify research topic/questions, narrow focus																														✓						
Use alphabetical order and key words, index				✓			✓				✓				✓	✓							✓			✓				✓						

115

© Incentive Publications, Inc., Nashville, TN

Use It! Don't Lose It! IP 612-4

ANSWER KEY

Week 1 (pages 5–7)
MONDAY
1. Apollo, Athena, and Poseidon are a few of the familiar gods and goddesses associated with Greek mythology; but Zeus was the god held in highest regard by the ancient Greeks.
2. strategies or skillful maneuvering
3. b
4. resign, cede, relinquish
5. Sentences will vary. One possible correct summary: Myths and legends both tell stories, but a myth usually tells about gods and goddesses, while a legend most often involves human behaviors.

TUESDAY
1. idiom
2. c
3. enraged
4. anti, contra
5. b

WEDNESDAY
1. Many responses are possible: something that has become popular (The song was an instant hit!); to come in contact with (He hit the ball with the bat.); to apply forcefully (Mom hit the brakes just in time.); to make a request of (He hit up his friend for a $10 loan.); to arrive or appear at (The best time to hit the stores is at the beginning of the day.); to bite at or on—fish (When I used salmon eggs I got three quick hits.); to reflect accurately (He hit the right note.); to deal another card (as in Blackjack); hit it big; hit it off; hit the fan; hit the ground running; hit the jackpot; hit the nail on the head.
2. The most powerful Greek gods lived atop Mount Olympus. There, on the mountaintop, the gods renewed their immortality, watched the games of mortal men, and discussed their concerns.
3. fiery, foreign, guarantee
4. The men seem to be protected and safe.
5. Student responses will vary. One possible correct response: Poseidon was angry with Zeus so he sent a flood to kill his brother's people. Zeus enlisted the help of the god of fire and saved the people using an unusual invention—the volcano.

THURSDAY
1. Pegasus's wings; Athena and Medusa's powers; horse's hooves
2. wisdom, love, courage
3. Odysseus traveled farther than anyone else to get to Ithaca.

4. atlas
5. Phrases will vary.

FRIDAY
1. Adjectives will vary. Six possible choices: independent, remarkable, skilled, self-assured, fast
2. Adjectives will vary. Six possible choices: resourceful, athletic, lucky, handsome, quick thinking, smitten
Writing will vary.

Week 2 (pages 8–10)
MONDAY
1. agree, consent, concur
2. who, which, whom, that
3. In, La Tomatina, At
4. asparagus, squashes or squash, potatoes, raspberries, celeries, bacon strips, shrimps or shrimp, escargots, grapefruit or grapefruits
5. Topic Sentence: Eating a healthy, well-balanced diet is one important step to living a long, healthy life. Details: 1) increased energy 2) excel in sports and academics 3) reduced occurrence of heart disease and cancer 4) live longer

TUESDAY
1. advise
2. b
3. also used in the manufacturing of dynamite
4. *whom*—objective; *their*—possessive; *they*—nominative; *she*—nominative
5. Paragraphs may vary. One possible combination: Bobby ate an onion-and-peanut-butter sandwich for breakfast and went to school without brushing his teeth. When Bobby greeted Frankie with a friendly "Hi, Buddy!", Frankie gagged at the smell of Bobby's breath and gave Bobby some mouthwash. Bobby doesn't eat onion-and-peanut-butter sandwiches anymore.

WEDNESDAY
1. limerick
2. Topic sentences will vary. One possible sentence: Unbelievable as it may seem, the Summer Lunch Program is both tasty and nutritious.
3. "Do you know how long the longest banana split was?" asked Jeff. "The people of Selinsgrove, Pennsylvania, do. They made a banana split that was 4.55 miles long."
4. The person making the statement is famished.
5. Stuffed! Features of the Day
   • Succulent seafood covered in a tangy mustard sauce. It will leave you wanting just one more bite!

   • Mouth-watering steaks grilled to perfection. A treat for your taste buds!
   • Delectable desserts—Sure to enhance your dining experience! Begin your amazing evening here!

THURSDAY
1. to ponder; to heat, sweeten, and flavor with spices; to pulverize
2. alliteration
3. declarative
4. butter
5. Statements of the main idea will vary. One possible interpretation: Today there are many varieties of candy chips on the market, but the original Toll House chocolate chips still rank among the tastiest.

FRIDAY
1. waffles, scrambled eggs, sausage
2. Student opinions will vary. Possible advantages include: Preparation is completed in advance, serving can be delayed and casserole kept warm in oven, tastes are mingled for a special treat.
3. Student opinions will vary. Possible disadvantages include: If you don't like one ingredient, the whole breakfast is ruined; cook must complete preparations in advance; waffles get soggy if not eaten promptly.
Writing may vary.
   1. Brown the sausage.
   2. Mix brown sugar and maple syrup.
   3. Pour over cooked sausage and keep warm in oven.
   4. Make waffles and scrambled eggs.
   5. Layer waffles, scrambled eggs, and sausages in casserole dish.
   6. Return to oven until time to eat.

Week 3 (pages 11–13)
MONDAY
1. Definitions will vary slightly. *Garrulous* means *talkative*.
2. Born Samuel Langhorne Clemens, Mark Twain grew up in Hannibal, Missouri, a small town on the west bank of the Mississippi River.
3. a
4. *Colloquial language* refers to the informal speech that people use in everyday conversation.
5. Responses will vary.

TUESDAY
1. con-, with, together; -ject, to throw; -ure, act or process; *Conjecture* means to guess or to form an opinion without definite evidence.
2. Answers will vary. Several correct answers are: narrated, described,

spun, expounded on, recounted
3. a. subject-verb agreement: The *characters personify* the injustices of a slaveholding society.
   b. subject-verb agreement: *Each brings* a unique perspective.
4. variety
5. When the Civil War broke out, the Mississippi River was closed to commercial traffic. Since riverboat pilots were no longer needed, Mark Twain ventured west to seek his fortune.

WEDNESDAY
1. *holy*—sacred; *holey*—having holes; *wholly*—completely, fully
2. Though his final books were filled with the depravity of human nature, Twain is chiefly remembered today for capturing the brash, optimistic spirit of Americans.
3. a. plural; b. single
4. more often; most often
5. Student should have drawn lines to the appropriate words.

THURSDAY
1. Explanations will vary. A habit is hard to break and it may be necessary to take small steps before the goal of eradication is achieved.
2. metaphor
3. Mark Twain's childhood home—Hannibal, Missouri—was a frequent stop for steamboats arriving from St. Louis and New Orleans.
4. Advice for Little Girls; The Celebrated Jumping Frog of Calaveras County
5. a. realistic, historical fiction; b. fantasy; c. science fiction

FRIDAY
1. There are many examples: ketched for caught; cal'klated for calculated; edercate for educate; never did nothing for never did anything; set for sit; learn for teach; got him up so in the matter of for became so good at; im for him. The storyteller ignores quotation marks and tends to speak in run-on sentences.
2. Student responses will vary. Smiley's frog can snatch flies off the counter and jump high. Wheeler says that the frog is modest and straightforward as well as talented.
3. Student opinions will vary.
Writing will vary.

Week 4 (pages 14–16)
MONDAY
1. Answers will vary. The iconography is the pictorial images associated or illustrating a subject.

2. Peanuts, upset, baseball, loses
3. The superlative form of early is earliest.
4. personification
5. Answers will vary. One possible response: The Katzenjammers combined both the aspects of internal dialogue and multi-panel cartoons, and so were pioneers in developing the form of the modern comic strip.

TUESDAY
1. Answers will vary. One possible answer: A comic strip is a sequence of cartoon drawings that tells a story.
2. In a famous comment on the ecological crisis, the comic-strip opossum Pogo said, "We have met the enemy, and he is us."
3. Answers will vary, but should reflect the idea that man is the cause of the ecological crisis.
4. Topics will vary. Check to make sure that the research questions address the topic given.
5. In 1924, the adventure strip was born. George Washington Tubbs II, the main character of a comic strip created by Roy Crane, embarked on a search for buried treasure. Readers were enthralled by the serial cliffhangers featuring Wash Tubbs.

WEDNESDAY
1. *Flagrant* means obviously inconsistent. Its connotation usually implies inconsistencies so serious that they cannot be condoned. The author of the sentence is probably not a liberal thinking individual.
2. The majority of traditional newspaper comic strips now have some Internet presence.
3. The sentence has a misplaced modifier. One possible correction: Frank King sometimes drew innovative backgrounds for his "Gasoline Alley" strip which first appeared in 1919.
4. *audience*: adults reading the editorial page of a newspaper; *purpose*: to illustrate a political opinion
5. The cartoon shows President Lincoln splitting a rail. In this case the rail represents the Democratic party.

THURSDAY
1. A caricature implies exaggeration of the characteristic features of a subject. So Walt Kelly caricatured Joseph McCarthy as a bobcat who considers himself omnipotent and

decides to get rid of undesirables in the birdwatching club, paralleling McCarthy's campaign to get rid of Communists in America.
2. Readers will often find political cartoons on the editorial page of the newspaper.
3. One possible answer: In 1897, the *New York Journal* published the first comic strip—"The Yellow Kid."
4. Opinions will vary. Check to make sure that students support their positions with details.
5. Some comic strips are centered on human beings, but a number of strips have animals as main characters. Some of the animals are nonverbal (Marmaduke), some have verbal thoughts but aren't understood by humans (Garfield, Snoopy), and some can converse with humans (Opus in "Bloom County" or Bucky and Satchel in "Get Fuzzy").

FRIDAY
1. Cells give living things form and function.
2. Personification: The animals talk and act like humans. Ask a question: The two questions "Why are cells so important?" and "So cells actually do things?" come before the main ideas.
3. Answers will vary. Current brain research supports this idea.
Cartoons will vary.

Week 5 (pages 17–19)
MONDAY
1. a. many—grow
   b. pincushion—stands
2. thorny, briery, troublesome, stinging
3. synonym
4. There are about 60 of the 3,000 cactus species growing in west Texas.
5. Sentences will vary. One possible correct summary: Cacti are well adapted to conditions with little rain. They have spines rather than water-wasting leaves, enlarged stems that store water, and extensive, close-to-the-surface root systems.

TUESDAY
1. boulders, stones, gravel, sand
2. on the pincushion cactus, of radial spines
3. The barrel cactus, fiercely armed with heavy spines, is one of the largest cacti of the North American deserts.
4. raven, rawhide, ravine
5. b

WEDNESDAY
1. Students will give different

meanings. Some correct examples: main stem of a plant; the long beam of a gun; the proprietorship element in a corporation usually divided into shares; liquid in which meat, fish, or vegetables have been simmered; an estimate or evaluation of something; confidence; to supply; to put in supplies
2. alliteration
3. stingy, trolley, rally, airy, subtle, or subtly
4. encyclopedia
5. Student responses will vary. One possible correct response: Information about the barrel cactus is succinct and clear cut in paragraph two. The same information is embedded in the personification of the cactus in passage one.

THURSDAY
1. The edible red pulp of the organ pipe cactus can be eaten as is, made into jelly, or fermented into a beverage.
2. confined
3. a. Who; b. whom
4. Student responses will vary. Check to make sure the sentence is complete and includes the details provided.
5. Student responses will vary. Check to see that the names suggested have a connection to the appearance of each cactus.

FRIDAY
1. The setting of the story is the home of Trysdale, a man who has just returned from the wedding of the lady he had hoped to marry. Trysdale, a handsome, well-dressed soldier, is preoccupied with regret over his failure to charm the young lady. He seems used to getting his way and is annoyed that she ignored his proposal of marriage.
2. The cause of the misunderstanding is the lady's belief that Trysdale understands Spanish.
3. Student opinions will vary.
Writing will vary.

Week 6 (pages 20–22)
MONDAY
1. In 1802 President Jefferson offered a challenge to his young assistant Meriwether Lewis.
2. A pirogue is a small boat. The word is French derived from the Spanish word *piragua* and the Caribbean word *piraua*.
3. Definitions may vary. *Fixing for a start* means *making preparations*.
4. affected

5. Responses may vary, but should include at least four of the following: find a route to the Pacific Ocean; measure latitude and longitude; draw maps; learn about tribes along the route; study languages, customs, and hunting practices; arrange Washington visits for interested chiefs; and take careful notes about climate, plant, and animal life of the different regions.

TUESDAY
1. Ocean in view! Oh, the joy!
2. after the long delay—adverbial clause; for the expedition—preposition phrase
3. red dye
4. b
5. a-3; b-1; c-5; d-2; e-4

WEDNESDAY
1. *Provoke* means to *stimulate* or *incite*. Statements about the connotation of the verb will vary depending on personal experience. One possible response: While *excite* and *stimulate* seem to have positive connotations, the connotation of *provoke* is more negative. I often think of someone provoking a fight.
2. On most days Captain Lewis walked along the shore with his dog Seaman by his side.
3. Lewis preserved hundreds of cuttings, seeds, plants, and flowers.
4. Writing will vary.
5. a. fact: Actual distances required to find game can be measured and documented.
   b. opinion: The general term difficult time can be interpreted in many different ways.
   c. fact: Actual species can be counted.
   d. opinion: A "should" statement implies judgment and therefore is an opinion.

THURSDAY
1. A participle is a verbal used as an adjective. A gerund is a verbal used as a noun.
2. Responses will vary. Meriwether Lewis, son of a Virginia planter, was born in 1774.
3. incidentally, succeed
4. b
5. Captions will vary.

FRIDAY
1. false
2. true
3. false
4. false
5. false
Writing will vary.

ANSWER KEY

Week 7 (pages 23–25)

MONDAY
1. Definitions will vary. Ray—*Math: one endpoint and all the points of a line on one side of the endpoint; Everyday: a fish with a flat body and eyes on one side*
Point—*Math: a location; Everyday: an individual detail*
2. lien
3.

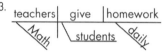

4. Responses will vary.
5. Responses may vary. One possible explanation: While the angles and sides of a congruent figure are equal or congruent, only the angles of similar figures are congruent and the lengths of their corresponding sides are proportional.

TUESDAY
1. *inter-* meaning between; *sec* meaning to cut; *-tion* meaning action of
2. Responses will vary. One correct response is *unsymmetrical.*
3. Ever since it was written in 400 B.C., Euclid's book <u>The Elements</u> has formed the basis for most of the geometry studied.
4. quadrilateral
5. Titles will vary. One possible title is Steps for Bisecting an Angle. Check to make sure that the title is properly capitalized.

WEDNESDAY
1. Sentences will vary. Two correct possibilities: Thomas drew the line segment on his paper. Thomas segmented the orange.
2. Coordinates; Coordinating; coordinates
3. Responses will vary, but should reflect the idea that some individuals are not suited to some situations.
4. who
5. Definitions will vary. One possible definition: two lines that lie in the same plane and have no points in common

THURSDAY
1. b
2. Definitions will vary. One possible definition: A polygon is a closed figure that has three or more line segments that do not cross.
3. Any polygon, regular or irregular, has as many angles as it has sides.
4. a. intersected; b. paralleled; c. admitted
5. a. translation or slide; b. rotation; c. reflection

FRIDAY
1. Opinions will vary.
2. False; Today's astronomers see the sun as the center of the solar system and the solar system as a small part of a galaxy in a larger universe.
3. Music, Mathematics, and Astronomy
Writing will vary.

Week 8 (pages 26–28)

MONDAY
1. Answers may vary slightly due to students' experiences: a. negative; b. positive; c. negative; d. neutral
2. William Faulkner was born into a prominent Southern family in Mississippi.
3. a. the blueberries' stain
b. the mosquitoes' bites
4. Responses will vary.
5. personification, metaphor, symbolism

TUESDAY
1. Sentences will vary. Influenced by his great-grandfather, who was an accomplished novelist, the young William Faulkner was an avid reader and devoured tales of the Civil War, folklore, French poetry, and Bible stories.
2. vindacate, obesety
3. In 1926 Faulkner tried his hand at fiction and published his first novel, *Soldiers' Pay.*
4. dictionary
5. a-2; b-1; c-4; d-3

WEDNESDAY
1. *Virulent* has several meanings: 1) marked by a destructive course—a virulent infection; 2) extremely poisonous; 3) very harsh—virulent criticism; 4) full of malice—virulent racists. Sentences will vary.
2. experimented
3. A flashback is an interruption of chronological sequence to show an event that happened earlier.
4. Phrases will vary. Faulkner found fame.
5. Responses will vary. Faulkner is describing afternoon teatime. His lines "Stiffly erect, decorous as to knee Among toy balloons of dignity on threads of talk" seem to say that the ritual of teatime is formal and rigid. The narrator is not comfortable as he sits among the "toy balloons" making small talk.

THURSDAY
1. Responses will vary.
2. William Faulkner, a Southerner himself, wrote about the conservative rural South.
3. *Temerity* means *rashness* or *contempt of danger.* Although *temerity* sounds a little like *timid,* a shy person would probably not demonstrate temerity.
4. Topics and questions will vary.
5. Sentences will vary. William Faulkner experimented with inconsistent punctuation; utilized repetition, long and puzzling sentences, and multiple points of view; and wrote in a stream-of-consciousness style.

FRIDAY
1. Faulkner is describing the carpenter Cash at work.
2. Cash is making a box to lie in—a casket.
3. Observations will vary, but should reference the long, entangled sentences, rich description, and the tendency to break grammar rules.
Writing will vary.

Week 9 (pages 29–31)

MONDAY
1. a. University of Arizona; b. U. of A.; c. K.S.U.; d. Florida State University; e. Lewis and Clark University; f. Stanford University
2. Neither hard work nor lack of sleep deters Benjamin.
3. pasttime, elegible, libary
4. An adverb clause is a subordinate clause that modifies a verb, an adjective, or an adverb. It tells when, where, how, why, to what extent, or under what conditions.
5. Although many high school students complain about how colleges evaluate applications, in the end the process is usually quite fair.

TUESDAY
1. business letter
2. Every period and comma was scrutinized.
3. efficient, disciplined, accommodating, conscientious, humorous, versatile
4. Whoever reads
5. Descriptions will vary.

WEDNESDAY
1. The subject and verb do not agree. Ignore an intervening expression between a subject and its verb. The verb must agree with the subject.
2. than–in comparison with; then–at that time
3. Colin Powell reported, "I was born in Harlem, raised in the South Bronx, went to public school, got out of public college, went into the Army, and then I just stuck with it."
4. In drama, a soliloquy is a long speech given by a character alone on stage. It usually reveals the private thoughts and emotions of the character.
5. Amherst College; The notes say that professors at Amherst spend less time on big research projects and more time in the classroom, so students there probably receive more personal attention. Science courses require lots of math; so a university that focuses on science, like MIT, would require more math.

THURSDAY
1. c
2. Each of the students writes an essay for his or her college application.
3. Hernando read the pamphlet about financial aid before filling out the questionnaire.
4. In my opinion, we should consider every suggestion.
5. statistic; fact; opinion; reason; example

FRIDAY
1. Definitions may vary. A tradition is an established behavior or action.
2. The *Sooners* were named for the homesteaders in the Oklahoma Land Run of 1889 who cheated and crossed the starting line early to get the best tracts of land.
3. At the University of Oklahoma the Sooner Schooner circles the field after each touchdown. University of Florida fans *chomp* their opponents with extended arms. Texas A&M students practice cheers at midnight.
4. College students rub both Testudo and the foot of the Statue of Three Lies for good luck.
Writing will vary.

Week 10 (pages 32–34)

MONDAY
1. at the same time
2. Born in Harlem during the Depression, James Baldwin overcame many hardships to produce a body of work that is acclaimed in American literature.
3. know for no; past for passed; too for the second to
4. Disillusioned about the prospect of social change in the United States
5. starving : hungry

TUESDAY
1. b
2. Sentences will vary. The trio developed the habit of hanging around the local drugstore to pass the time; they called it browsing, the shop owner saw it as loitering.
3. James Baldwin's first novel, *Go Tell It on the Mountain,* was published in

1953 and became an important portrait of life in the United States.

4. title of novel, author, city of publication, publisher, year of publication
5. Explanations will vary.

WEDNESDAY
1. a
2. A foil is a character who is used as a contrast with a second character. The purpose of a foil is to highlight a particular quality of the second character.
3. Definitions will vary. *Uncompromising realism* means he pulled no punches; he told it like it is.
4. Sentences will vary. My English teacher requires that I formally introduce my parents at Parent-Teacher Conferences. Sizzling Steaks was formerly called The Great T-Bone.
5. Opinions will vary.

THURSDAY
1. The second phrase is a sentence fragment. Possible corrections—
1) Add a verb to make the sentence complete: His anger was apparent.
2) Combine the phrase with the first sentence: He left, his anger apparent, without saying good-bye.
2. Explanations will vary. The statement means that James Baldwin was an expressive and forceful voice protesting racial inequality.
3. absence, accidentally, accommodate, a lot
4. thesaurus
5. Sentences will vary. James Baldwin, the grandson of slaves, was raised in Harlem by a stern stepfather during economic hard times.

FRIDAY
1. *Raised a song* means *began to play*. It might be considered a dialect, colloquial language, local color, or an idiom.
2. Suggested words may vary: anticipation, ceremony, memory
3. Explanations will vary, but should reference the use of "almost" antonyms to effectively describe a feeling. The second pair of words—belief, real.
Descriptions will vary.

Week 11 (pages 35–37)
MONDAY
1. The subject (team) and the adjective (their) don't agree. The team can't change its score after the buzzer.
2. eligable, balet, hygeine
3. a. athletic; b. athletics; c. athlete's

4. Repetition
5. In 1865 the record was about 4 min 36 sec. In 1923 the record was 4 min. 10 sec. The difference is 16 seconds.

TUESDAY
1. Peanut-butter-and-jelly sandwiches are favorites among hungry skiers.
2. a. passed; b. past
3. Sentences will vary. Coaches and assistant coaches teach football players and wrestlers useful strategies.
4. Sentences will vary. Putting pads on the floor is an important step in keeping wrestlers injury-free.
5. Summaries will vary.
You can use the Dewey Decimal System to help find a book in a library. Each book is given a number that tells what the book is about. Any book on the arts is part of the 700s. Recreation books are considered a part of arts and are labeled 790. Outdoor games is a subtopic of recreation and so a book about outdoor games is further classified as 796. Adding a decimal point and more numbers defines additional categories. For example, a book about outdoor games requiring equipment is labeled 796.2.

WEDNESDAY
1. a. There, in the display case, are five prize trophies.
b. Waiting here in the gym are the members of the winning team.
2. have
3. Antonyms may vary. a. agree; b. awkwardness; c. unmotivated; d. flexible; e. selfish; f. irrigate
4. The comparison is a metaphor. The sentence also includes imagery and explicit verbs.
5. Comparisons will vary.

THURSDAY
1. Score is singular.
2. Who
3. changeable
4. magazines, journals, newspapers, newsletters
5. a. Chairs rocked back and forth as swimmers filed in and out of the noisy, cramped staging area.
b. In a sea of oiled bodies and latex swim caps, Mark sat with seven other swimmers. He felt tense and tried to relax.
c. When the clerk called Mark's heat, he scrubbed his hands on his sweatshirt, pulled the shirt over his head, adjusted his goggles, and walked toward the blocks with confidence.

FRIDAY
1. bade—asked that, the past tense of bid: doffed—removed, *doffed his hat* can be a sign of respect or a salute; awed—quieted (inspired with awe); wonderment—astonishment, surprise; favored—special; maddened—crazed, enraged
2. Responses will vary. A tongue can applaud by shouting congratulations.
3. Responses will vary. A runner hugs third by staying close to third base.
4. Responses will vary. Blake hit the baseball hard.
Writing will vary.

Week 12 (pages 38–40)
MONDAY
1. While in Chicago I hope to see The Drowsy Chaperone, Hairspray, and The Producers.
2. The subject is an implied *you*.
3. Attributes may vary. A play is a story that has been written to be performed for an audience.
• story told through actions and words of the characters
• includes dialogue, stage directions
• may be comedy or tragedy
• usually divided into acts and scenes
4. deserted dive
5. Definitions will vary.
onstage—on a part of the stage visible to the audience
apron—the part of the stage in front of the curtain or proscenium arch
cue—a signal to a performer to begin a specific speech or action
house—the audience in a theater
set—the artificial setting for a scene of a theatrical production
wings—the area at the side of a stage out of sight

TUESDAY
1. The two men rewrote Victor Hugo's novel in a new form for the theater.
2. *Rent* (a study of young hungry artists in New York City's East Village) is a modern interpretation of the opera *La Boheme*.
3. director, manager, operator
4. Opinions will vary.
5. All are citations used to document information in research writing.
parenthetical documentation—the author's name and a page reference in parentheses after the information from that author.
footnotes—a reference at the bottom of the text page that contains the citation; Footnotes are numbered and match a superscript number following the information in the text.

endnotes—Endnotes are similar to footnotes; however, endnote citations appear on a separate page at the end of a paper instead of on the page with the documented material.

WEDNESDAY
1. climax
2. A protagonist is the central character in a literary work. Generally, the audience is meant to sympathize with the protagonist.
3. The Crucible dramatizes the story of an historical incident in Seventeenth-Century Salem, Massachusetts, in which accusations made by a young woman set off a witch-hunt.
4. threat
5. April 5; 6:30 p.m.; $25.00; Johnson Theater—TPAC; Row A, seat 14

THURSDAY
1. The playwright may be a woman so "his" should not be used.
• A playwright must make careful word choices in his or her work.
• Playwrights must make careful word choices in their work.
• Making careful word choices is important to a playwright.
2. Stage directions explain how characters should look, speak, act, and move on the stage.
3. A monologue is a long speech by a character in a literary work.
4. 3, 5, 2, 6, 4, 1
5. Students should make an X on the bottom left corner of the Orchestra Section K–R.

FRIDAY
1. Opinions may vary. Both *The Lion King* and *Oklahoma* are acceptable choices.
2. musicals, Broadway shows
3. Adjectives may vary. Rosie Herman—effortless, agile, successful; John Robertson—sloppy, gravelly, disappointing; Lily Moon—spunky, innocent, blossoming; Scott Carpenter—amusing, slapstick, singing
4. A theatrical review is personal-expressive writing. It may also be considered persuasive and descriptive.
5. Opinions and writing will vary.

Week 13 (pages 41–43)
MONDAY
1. Species that receive protection under the ESA are classified into two categories, "Endangered" or "Threatened," depending on their status and how severely their survival is threatened.

ANSWER KEY

2. Who
3. "Ever since before the beginning of recorded history," Jan Goble suggests, "man has played a decisive role in the quality of his environment and the loss of life in it."
4. reptile, frugal
5. Statements of the main idea will vary. The gorilla population is close to extinction due to commercial hunting and an outbreak of Ebola.

TUESDAY
1. beyond or beside
2. Thesis statements will vary.
3. The shady pursuit of endangered bird eggs made international headlines when Colin Watson, widely considered Britain's most notorious egg collector, died after falling from a 12-meter tree while hunting a rare egg.
4. Diamond, Jared. *The Third Chimpanzee: The Evolution and Future of the Human Animal.* Chicago: Harper Perennial, 1992.
5. A secondary consumer in the food chain is a carnivore that eats herbivores.

WEDNESDAY
1. Several possible synonyms are: threatened, imperiled, and jeopardized.
2. two rhinos' horns; two beetles' shells; two t-rexes' roars
3. effects
4. 2, 3, 1, 4 or 3, 1, 2, 4
5. Poe uses an elaborate, rhythmic rhyme scheme that uses internal rhyme within a single line, repetition of the rhyming words, and end rhyme as well.
Once upon a midnight <u>dreary</u>/ while I pondered, weak and <u>weary</u>, (a, a)
Over many a quaint and curious/ volume of forgotten <u>lore</u>, (b)
While I nodded, nearly <u>napping</u>,/ suddenly there came a <u>tapping</u>, (c, c)
As of someone gently <u>rapping</u>,/ <u>rapping</u> at my chamber <u>door</u>. (c, c, b)
"'Tis some visitor," I muttered,/ "<u>tapping</u> at my chamber <u>door</u>—/ Only this, and nothing <u>more</u>."c, b, b

THURSDAY
1. Each of the animals has specific requirements for survival.
2. The word *endangered* was recognized by *Webster* as a "new" word in 1964.
3. *Incredible* means unbelievable, while *incredulous* means skeptical.
4. Research topics and questions will vary. Check to see that the topics

are appropriately limited in scope.
5. a. opinion; b. fact; c. fact

FRIDAY
1. the moon or some other nightly traveler in the sky
2. Responses will vary. The observer respects and admires the magnificent cat.
3. The observer seems to disapprove of the changes in the cat's environment. The connotation of descriptive words are negative when referring to humans (chaotic) and positive when referring to the tiger (magnificence).
4. portentous—impressive, prodigious; abundant—ample, abounding; forays—raids; domain—territory
Descriptions will vary.

Week 14 (pages 44–46)
MONDAY
1. light/shadow; sharp/blunt; small/big; annihilation/rebirth
2. In traditional Balinese mythology, Batara Kala is the god of the underworld and the creator of the light and the earth.
3. complex
4. *Annihilate* means *nullify* or *destroy*.
5. Summaries will vary. Using antonym examples, Minke suggests that change is inevitable. He sees life as a never-ending cycle.

TUESDAY
1. Because the exchange rate changes continually and the Internet can best keep up with the changes, it is the best reference.
2. indigenous, simple, inborn, natural
3. puppeteer; paradise; humidity
4. Punctuate with a dash to indicate a sudden break or change in the sentence or to emphasize a word, series of words, phrase or clause.
5. Interpretations may vary.
   a. The people of Aceh, who suffered losses due to a tsunami, are glad at least that their country is at peace.
   b. The person responsible for bombing the embassy is found guilty and sent to jail.
   c. The heads of state of different countries in Asia are campaigning for ways to eliminate air pollution.

WEDNESDAY
1. metaphor
2. am
3. A Tok Dalang is the puppet master in traditional Wayang Kulit.
4. Hindus
5. Students may explain the meaning differently. Mr. Geary believes that injustices of the 19th century

imperialists have been passed on to become accepted 20th century practices. He uses the Indonesian writer Pramoedya as an example. Pramoedya wrote a novel about injustice while imprisoned as an alleged subversive.

THURSDAY
1. shadow puppets
2. Wayang kulit are Indonesian puppets with movable, jointed arms.
3. true
4. Opinions may vary. The words and phrases chosen by the author create a positive feeling or mood. (playfulness, charming simplicity, spellbinding medium)
5. Wayang Puppetry
   • a traditional Indonesian puppet play lasts about seven hours
   • gongs, drums, and xylophones provide background music
   • beautiful leather puppets are neatly arranged, their body-sticks firmly planted in banana stems
   • good character on the right-hand side, bad on the left
   • the play begins with a knock on the puppet chest

FRIDAY
1. Each line is a fact. Some of the facts include:
   • The nation of Indonesia is located in the Pacific Ocean.
   • Indonesian has more than 17,000 islands.
   • 6,000 of Indonesia's islands are uninhabited.
   • Indonesia is the world's fourth most populous nation.
   • The national language of Indonesia is Bahasa Indonesia.
   • The capital of Indonesia is Jakarta.
   • Eight million people live in Jakarta.
2. Word choices will vary. One possible choice might be diversity. Indonesia's people, geography, and cultures reflect diversity.
3. Sentences will vary. Indonesia faces frequent earthquakes, volcanic eruptions, and tsunamis; here, in Tennessee, common natural disasters are limited to local floods, tornadoes, or ice storms.
4. *Takes to heart* means to consider seriously. Outlines will vary.

Week 15 (pages 47–49)
MONDAY
1. intransitive
2. a
3. Words given will vary. Make sure that they are precise.

4. *Agape* means *wide open*.
5. Preposterous! Irresistible! Unthinkable! Absolutely Not!

TUESDAY
1. *Inedible* should be *incredible*
2. Opening sentences will vary.
3. *The Guinness Book of World Records*
4. cook it
5. conjecture–proof; wicked–virtuous; boorish–polite; arrogance–modesty; hovel–castle; elude–confront

WEDNESDAY
1. suspend
2. The fans in the stands booed the football players.
3. he
4. Words will vary. Several possible choices: enthusiastic—burst; angry—charged
5. Start by kneeling or lying on the surfboard. Paddle out to the area beyond the breaking waves. Wait for the right wave. When you see one coming, turn and paddle furiously toward the shore. If you time it right, the wave will pick up your surfboard and carry it along. Stand up on the board and ride it down the vertical face of the wave.

THURSDAY
1. *Obstreperous* means unruly. While some skateboarders may be obstreperous, being unruly is not an attribute required for skateboarding.
2. subject—tumbling; direct object—what
3. In the marathon leg of the 1989 Ironman Triathlon in Hawaii, Jim MacLaren, a 27-year-old professional triathlete and a former linebacker for Yale, fell in step with 41-year-old Ken Mitchell, who played the same position for the Atlanta Falcons.
4. No. *Enervated* means lacking physical, mental, and moral vigor. A marathon runner must have physical and mental vigor.
5. 27, 49-50, 51, 151

FRIDAY
1. Answers will vary. Whitewater rafting is one possibility.
2. A gerund is a verb form that ends in –ing and is used as a noun.
3. Answers will vary. Hoarse-voice cheering is one correct answer.
4. It begins quickly, slows to a meander, speeds up and builds in intensity, and then slows down once again.
5. Synonyms will vary. meander—wander, wind; narrow—taper, constrict; pacify—appease, calm;

satisfy—please, gratify
Poems will vary.

Week 16 (pages 50–52)
MONDAY
1. Sentences will vary. Scurrying onto the train, the passengers looked liked ants rushing back to the anthill from a picnic.
2. personification
3. The author has coined the phrase "age in place" to parallel "march in place". A soldier who marches in place marches, but doesn't move. The older citizens the sentence refers to grow older in their communities; they don't have to move to retirement communities.
4. Congestion and traffic problems are no longer confined to the largest metropolitan areas.
5. Observations will vary.

TUESDAY
1. Topics will vary. Check to see that the topics have an appropriately narrow scope.
2. It's a run-on sentence.
3. "It seems imperative," reports Richard J. Jackson, M.D., "that new transportation options be developed and implemented in order to help alleviate the public health problems related to worsening air quality."
4. Responses will vary—a new route, a new light rail, free rides, road construction.
5. Summaries will vary. One possible summary: Individuals 65 and older see a need for more public transportation in their communities because they believe that it is safer than driving alone and provides easy access to their everyday needs.

WEDNESDAY
1. A ballad is a narrative song or poem. Folk ballads, which usually tell an exciting story, were passed down by word of mouth for generations before being written down.
2. Sentences will vary. My parents have always parked in the commuter lot.
3. intersection, benefits
4. Responses will vary.
5. The phrase get on board means to board or climb into or onto a vehicle. If you get on board in this instance you recognize that riding public transportation saves energy costs. Public transportation is compared to a key. Opinions on the effectiveness of the slogan will vary.

THURSDAY
1. buses, ferries, trolleys, taxis
2. arrives
3. Responses will vary, but should reference the use of blunting and crippling which carry negative connotations.
4. The refrain tells the story of a man who spent his entire life riding the subway beneath Boston because he didn't have the money to pay the fare to exit the train.
5. Statements of the main idea will vary. Researchers suggest that some commuters get more than 30 minutes of walking on days when they ride public transit.

FRIDAY
1. six; one
2. They are determined by whether the rider purchases a single or round trip.
3. Individual ride prices would mount up fast—$882. Buying weekly passes (only $85 per week) would save money.
4. Suggestions will vary.
Persuasive paragraphs will vary.

Week 17 (pages 53–55)
MONDAY
1. receipt, misspell
2. His mother said, "Quit talking foolishness!"
3. a. affected; b. effect
4. Colloquial language is informal speech that people use in everyday conversation.
5. spying—intelligence gathering; retreat—strategic withdrawal; fire—terminate

TUESDAY
1. passed
2. An interrogative sentence is one that asks a question.
3. No. The statement is common knowledge that would appear in most sources on the fair.
4. Details will vary, but should reference the many quirks and exceptions in the English language.
5. a. a well-oiled bicycle
   b. a crushing blow

WEDNESDAY
1. Carl Sandburg compares slang to a working man. Student opinions will vary.
2. argument; When adding a suffix to words ending in e, usually drop the e.
3. Abstract language is language that expresses an idea or intangible reality, as opposed to a specific object or occurrence. Safety,

happiness, and courage are examples of abstract language.
4. speak, spoke, has spoken; write, wrote, has written
5. Interpretations will vary. A patient knight waited with sword in hand. A creature, the Jabberwock, emerged from the wood. The knight slew the beast, left it dead, and returned triumphantly with the beast's head.

THURSDAY
1. A summary paper explores a topic by summing up the opinions of other writers. The author of the paper does not express an opinion about the subject. An evaluative paper states an opinion and backs it up with evidence found in primary and secondary sources. An original paper is based on the writer's own original research—for example, observation, experimentation, interviews. It leads to new insights or information about the topic.
2. Words will vary.
3. series; blackberries; attorneys general
4. essential adjective clause
5. a temperature scale—Gabriel Fahrenheit; unit of electricity—James Watt; a wind instrument—Adolphe Sax

FRIDAY
1. raining cats and dogs—raining hard or in great amounts; green thumb—knack of growing plants; an arm and a leg—a lot of money; every cloud has a silver lining—there is something good even in an unpleasant situation; a blue ribbon winner—top prize recipient; don't count your chickens before they hatch—don't plan on something before it occurs; on pins and needles—worried or excited about something; dime a dozen—commonly available; the cat's meow—the latest thing or style; picking and hauling—working hard; the day pigs fly—it will never happen
2. Interpretations may vary. The setting is a garden probably on a rural farm or in a small town at least 50 years ago.
3. Check to see students have added appropriate details to the Venn diagrams.
Student writing will vary.

Week 18 (pages 56–58)
MONDAY
1. During his lifetime, Robert Frost received more awards (including four Pulitzer Prizes for Poetry and a

Congressional medal) than any other twentieth-century poet.
2. preferred
3. Superficial means shallow or concerned only with the obvious.
4. Responses will vary.
5. a–b–a–a–b–c–b–c–b

TUESDAY
1. When Frost returned from England, prominent publishers backed his work and America's most prestigious universities invited him to teach in their schools.
2. William H. Pritchard, Frost: A Literary Life Reconsidered (New York: Oxford University Press, 1984) 83.
3. Sentence combinations will vary. Robert Frost was born in San Francisco and lived there until his father died when he was 12. Then he moved to Massachusetts.
4. Dialogue is the conversation between characters in a literary work.
5. Rued means regretted.

WEDNESDAY
1. At age 26, Frost moved to a farm near Derry, New Hampshire, where he got to know the inhabitants of rural New England.
2. An appositive phrase is an appositive plus any other words that modify the appositive. An appositive is a noun or pronoun that is placed next to another noun or pronoun to identify or give information about it. In the sentence Robert Frost, the American poet, was a prolific writer, the phrase the American poet is an appositive phrase.
3. Attributes may vary. Historical fiction has a setting that represents a real time and place, the characters in the story may have been real people, and the story includes actual historical events.
4. a. finally modifies ending;
   b. quite modifies deep;
   c. almost modifies never;
   d. tomorrow modifies shovel
5. Responses will vary. In my car I would not hear the sweep of the wind and downy flake. The description appeals to my sense of hearing. It creates a quiet, peaceful mood.

THURSDAY
1. In this sentence, embedded means it has become a part of the American imagination.
2. a. dipping; b. repelling; c. resetting; d. developing; e. training
3. Questions will vary.

ANSWER KEY

4. Student writing will vary, but should include time and place references.
5. Responses will vary.

FRIDAY
1. The speaker's property is an apple orchard, while the other man's property is a pine forest.
2. The speaker doesn't believe that the wall is necessary and therefore sees the repair of the wall as an unnecessary activity, a "game".
3. Since some of the stones in the wall are round, it is hard to make them balance on one another. The phrase *use a spell to make them balance* is like saying, "I have to hold my mouth just right."
4. No, the man with the pine forest believes that walls and fences are necessary. The speaker questions their purpose and the necessity for keeping them repaired.
5. Comparisons will vary. The poem explores a paradox in human nature: that we want a wall, a barrier to protect ourselves from others, but also need that wall to break down so we can interact with others. The poem explores how and why we erect barriers between ourselves. When the wall is broken and the speaker and the neighbor repair it, they are in contact — "we walk the line", and when the wall is fixed, it is back to their individual lives and "I" and "he". Frost sees the futility of the wall and questions the necessity of the wall.
   Student writing will vary. Check to see that the writing supports the position expressed.

Week 19 (pages 59–61)
MONDAY
1. Each capitalized word in the following sentence should have three short underlines on the original copy. Baron Pierre de Coubertin was the founder of the modern Olympic games.
2. The coach told the gymnast to learn a new vault.
3. forfeit
4. a. snatch; b. clean and jerk
5. Sentences will vary. The inspiration for the modern pentathlon was a 19th-century French cavalry officer who rode a horse, fought a duel, ran, and swam across a river in order to deliver his message.

TUESDAY
1. When you revise you review and evaluate your draft to make sure that it accomplishes its purpose and speaks to its intended audience.

Revising is about content and word choice, organization, and flowing sentences.
2. Tug of war, rugby, polo, lacrosse, power boating, and golf have all been Olympic events.
3. The International Olympic Committee (IOC) is an international nonprofit organization.
4. The sport is fencing. One synonym for *rivals* is *competitors*. One synonym for *feint* is *trick*.
5. Sentences will vary. At the start of the course, the slider accelerated by paddling with spiked gloves.

WEDNESDAY
1. signals
2. hurdler
3. Illustrations should show one arrow splitting the shaft of a second arrow already embedded in the target.
4. Opinions will vary but should be supported with logical reasons.
5. When the game was first played, table tennis rackets were cigar-box lids, but players today use rubber-coated wooden rackets that are specially developed for hitting the lightweight ball.

THURSDAY
1. Capitalize proper adjectives (adjective formed from proper nouns).
2. Olympic competitors, passers-by
3. Before the race began, the newscasters enjoyed telling the athletes' stories.
4. Many sources would include the information. An Internet search would probably be the most efficient.
5. Explanations should point out the contrast between the meaning of the word and the sport. While the word *judo* means *the gentle way*, it is the only Olympic sport where submission holds allow choking an opponent or breaking an arm—certainly not *gentle* moves.

FRIDAY
1. A flashback is an interruption in the chronological order of a narrative to show an event that happened earlier.
2. The majority of sentences in the selection are part of a flashback. Sentences not highlighted are the first three sentences in the first paragraph, the first line of the second paragraph, the first two sentences of the last paragraph, "And the rockets' red glare…", and the final two sentences.
3. touch—graze, rubbed;

hearing—strain, quiets, ring; sight—unfurls, spot
4. Old Glory is personified as it ascends the pole.
5. The excerpt takes place at an Olympic awards ceremony.

Week 20 (pages 62–64)
MONDAY
1. The noun *currency* has several meanings. a) a medium of exchange; b) prevalence; c) state of being current
2. Those who collect currency are generally referred to as "numismatists".
3. England is also known as Great Britain—Great Britain Pound.
4. Student responses will vary.
5. Details may vary, but might include: has value in more than one country is easily carried can be easily measured is available to West Africans

TUESDAY
1. cent—a coin representing a monetary unit—1/100 of the main unit; scent—a distinctive odor
2. Foreign traders didn't want to spend hours negotiating every transaction with weights and scales.
3. fact
4. €193.45
5. Notes may vary. How collective currency is valued:
   • subjective appearance:coloration, centering, finish, wear
   • objective factors: date issued, series, mint/print location, ink colors, number issues, rarity

WEDNESDAY
1. Never lay down valuable possessions. Monitor belongings carefully.
2. Complete subject: The capacity to convert perishable commodities into money; Simple subject: capacity
3. A thesis is the main idea of a work of nonfiction. It may be stated directly or implied.
4. The advantages and disadvantages students suggest will vary. *Advantages*—can be valued, is measurable, not perishable, strong *Disadvantages*—size (difficult to fit into pocket, heavy), difficult to manufacture, requires ready supply of copper; hard to store
5. a magnifying glass; ruler; bright white light; pricing guide

THURSDAY
1. Many requirements might be listed: portable—can fit in a pocket; lightweight; nonperishable—won't

rot; strong and durable—won't crush, rip, crack, break off, or bend out of shape; can get wet without being ruined; can be produced in standard sizes so that any two pieces are identical; can be marked or made in different sizes to show different values (such as $1, $5, or $10 bill); can be easily stacked or stored; cannot be forged, adulterated, or thinned to lessen its value; supply is large enough to be available to everyone; supply is limited enough to preserve its value; all users believe in its value and agree to trade with it
2. You want general ideas.
3. No, it does not have value beyond its use as money.
4. Responses may vary. *buy*: S—purchase, A—sell; *request*: S—demand, A—reply; *courtesy*: S—civility, A—disrespect
5. Birr, Dalasia, Dinar, Euro, Koruna, Kroon, Kuna, Kwacha, Lek, Leva, Peso, Quetzal, Real, Rial, Ringgit, Rupee Rupiah, Taka

FRIDAY
1. A fiscal policy is a policy relating to taxation, public revenues, or public debt.
2. The formation of a common currency system in Europe required the cooperation, trust, and planning of many different countries. For the member countries to give up their own currency and accept the regional currency was a significant change—a major step.
3. Unlike the U.S. dollar there are no 1- or 2-euro bills. All bills are brightly colored and vary in size depending on their value.
4. Summaries may vary. The introduction of the euro has eased travel and commerce within Europe. The people of Europe seem to share a common bond attributable to the ease in travel and the common price levels.
Slogans will vary.

Week 21 (pages 65–67)
MONDAY
1. missing LINK
2. More than one answer is possible. canoe–ocean; reserve–reverse; robed–bored
3. time
4. stop sign; dare devils
5. Answers will vary. Some possibilities: pride, aged, drag, bread, caged, pager, idea, cried, acre, pacer, paced, bride, grade,

race, griped, price, pared, raged, brag, brigade, grace, graced, priced

TUESDAY
1. Seneca said, "Human affairs are like a chess game; only those who do not take it seriously can be called good players."
2. Checkmate is a winning move in chess where an opponent's king is trapped.
3. The castling move is a defensive maneuver where two chess pieces are moved during the same play. It speeds up the game of chess.
4. The first official world chess champion, Wilhelm Steinitz, claimed his title in 1886.
5. Opinions will vary. Check to see that the thesis statement expresses a position and that the examples cited support that position.

WEDNESDAY
1. In the early 1930s, Alfred Butts created a board-less game he called Lexico that was the predecessor to another of his games—Scrabble.
2. Responses may vary—indignant.
3. melody, song, musical phrase
4. Sentences will vary. Perusing the board to find a play, I stumbled across a triple-word-bonus word.
5. melinchoy, mogle, las, Li is a symbol for lithium, but not a word.

THURSDAY
1. *A monopoly on miscues* would be a monopoly on mistakes. Student opinions on whether they would like to be the only one making mistakes may vary.
2. World records are maintained for the longest game played in a treehouse (286 hours), underground (100 hours), in a bathtub (99 hours), and upside-down (36 hours).
3. Most foreign editions of Monopoly adopt their own currency and property names; for example, Boardwalk becomes Mayfair in England, Rue de la Paix in France, and Schlossallee in Germany.
4. through Web resources
5. Sentences will vary.

FRIDAY
Across 2. glossary; 4. plural;
    5. metaphor; 11. onomatopoeia;
    12. genre; 13. hyperbole; 14. fiction;
    15. homonym; 16. oxymoron
Down 1. tone; 3. alliteration;
    6. superlative; 7. simile;
    8. preamble; 9. conjunction;
    10. conclusion
Lists will vary.

Week 22 (pages 68–70)
MONDAY
1. Capitalize the first word in the closing.
2. Student responses will vary.
3. Amazingly, I've read your book four times and learned something new every time.
4. The second thesis is more persuasive because it is limited in scope and includes details (violent, nightmares) so that it is more believable.
5. A business letter includes an inside address in addition to the return address and date. The greeting is more formal and is punctuated with a colon in the business letter.

TUESDAY
1. a. friendly; b. business; c. business; d. friendly
2. Sentences will vary. Before I was halfway through with my salad, my brother had finished all of his dinner.
3. true
4. Addresses will vary, but should follow the proper format.
5. • Identify your purpose.
    • State your central claim clearly.
    • Present evidence in a logical sequence.
    • Explain how your evidence supports your claim.
    • Conclude by reaffirming your claim.

WEDNESDAY
1. *letter*—a communication addressed to a particular organization or person; a symbol representing a particular sound in a language; an award (consisting of the initial letter of the name of a school) for excellence, especially in varsity sports.
note—something written down, often in abbreviated form, as a record or reminder; a short written message; a sound of a particular pitch, quality, or duration; a symbol representing a sound; a black or white key of a piano or other keyboard instrument; a short written comment in the margin; a promissory note.
stamp—a small piece of gummed paper that is stuck on an envelope or package to show that postage has been paid; a small block with a raised design or lettering that can be printed onto paper by inking the block and pressing it to the paper; to suppress or eradicate something or somebody.
2. Dear Dr. Crawford:
3. *Claude* (clawed) *Severely* is

particularly appropriate for an ex-lion tamer since its meaning may tell the reason the animal trainer is an *ex*-animal trainer.
4. A paraphrase is a restatement of someone else's ideas in your own words. A summary is a short statement of the main ideas of a speech or piece of writing.
5. a. The correspondence represents an unofficial line of communication between two heads of state and as such carries benefits such as allowing the two leaders to get to know each other, discuss possible solutions privately, anticipate reactions, warn the other party about planned developments, etc.
    b. Eisenhower agreed with every word in the letter. He says that even if he wanted to disagree he was unable to find a way to do it.

THURSDAY
1. *Stationery* refers to the paper used in writing letters. *Stationary* means not moving or fixed in position.
2. Sincerely,
3. Analogies may vary; any response that indicates a long formal piece of writing, such as a treatise, is correct.
4. confused or puzzled
5. A hyperbole uses exaggeration to express strong emotion, to make a point, or to evoke humor. Abraham Lincoln was poking fun at his own appearance by saying that he realized that he was the ugliest man in the world.

FRIDAY
1. Definitions may vary. A kindred spirit is someone who shares a similarity of character or interests.
2. Robert Frost
    • participated in Kennedy's inauguration
    • born in CA
    • spent time at Harvard
    • 26 honorary degrees
    • taught at Amherst, Univ. of MI, Dartmouth, Harvard
    • lived in England and traveled internationally
3. The letter writer borrows the words "a time to talk" and "road less traveled by" from Frost's poetry. This "borrowing" differs from the everyday speech example because the use of the borrowed words is intentional to honor Frost and to demonstrate a familiarity with his poetry.
Student writing will vary.

Week 23 (pages 71–73)
MONDAY
1. Sentences may vary. One possible combination: The American Civil War was a separatist conflict between the U.S. Federal government and 11 states that seceded from the U.S. to form the Confederate States of America.
2. The sentence uses *bearly* instead of the correct word *barely*.
3. *secession*—a formal withdrawal from an organization, state, or alliance; *casualties*—a person or thing injured, lost, or destroyed; *confederate*—one of two or more people, groups, or nations that have formed an alliance for some common purpose
4. crises
5. a. "When Johnny Comes Marching Home"; b. Gilmore's Band; c. Union Army and Navy; d. 1863 in Boston

TUESDAY
1. *re-*: again as in retell, or back as in recall; *inforce* (a variant of *enforce*) so *en-*: means to put into; *force*: energy or strength); *-ment*: result of action or process. Reinforcement: the act or process of being reinforced; personnel or equipment sent to support a military action
2. Details may vary. Two possible inferences: a. Plantation owners needed slaves; b. People who favored secession favored slavery.
3. The Union, led by President Abraham Lincoln, opposed the expansion of slavery and rejected any right of secession.
4. Not necessarily; a fanatical belief is marked by excessive enthusiasm and often intense, uncritical devotion.
5. Additional details may be included, but the summary should include these ideas. The map shows the Battlefield of Shiloh near Pittsburgh Landing in Tennessee. It shows the position of U. S. soldiers. It was drawn after a survey on April 6 and 7, 1862. One inch on the map equals 1,200 feet.

WEDNESDAY
1. Union advantages in geography, manpower, industry, finance, political organization, and transportation overwhelmed the Confederacy.
2. Interpretations will vary. The singer is singing a song to the "Beautiful Dreamer." He asks her to awake, put aside everyday cares, and listen while he woos her with a soft melody.

ANSWER KEY

3. ode—an elaborate lyric poem expressed in a dignified and sincere way
4. When two parties agree on something, they both have the responsibility to uphold the agreement.
5. A Casus Belli is an event or action that justifies a war or conflict.

THURSDAY
1. Sentences may vary. On February 9, 1861, before Lincoln took office, seven states declared their secession from the Union and established a new government, the Confederate States of America.
2. Keywords will vary. Three possible words: Confederate, Union, War Between the States
3. *Intervene* means to interfere; to come in or between, e.g., to intervene to stop a fight.
4. Thomas Jefferson wrote a document declaring that all men were equal while he and others who signed the document owned slaves.
5. A. Civil War Issues: abolition, slavery
   B. Major Battles: Antietam, Pickett's Charge, Shiloh, Franklin
   C. Aftermath of Civil War: Reconstruction, 13th Amendment

FRIDAY
1. Responses may vary. The journal writer is a Union soldier who respects the Confederate soldiers that he faces. He is weary of war, questions its purpose, and is thankful to be alive.
2. Any writing during the period of the Civil War tended to be formal. The language of the time reflected a formality. The author chose formal words to make the journal entry authentic.
3. a. except for my blistered, tired feet
   b. experienced one victory
4. The author uses repetition of the word *another*. The rhythm of the word seems to echo the soldiers' marching feet and the hopelessness of the war.
   Attributes of historical fiction: The setting represents a real time; the setting represents a real place; characters in the story could have been or were real people; the story is about actual historical events. Opinions may vary.
   A Civil War soldier could have written the journal entry.

Week 24 (pages 74–76)
MONDAY
1. Antarctica; emergency; schedule

2. descriptive, persuasive
3. a place to which one is journeying
4. The speaker enthusiastically advocated international travel asserting, "All who travel overseas learn quickly that understanding and tolerance are fostered by common experience."
5. Critiques will vary, but should mention the negative reference to *beach-blanket peddlers* that *badger* tourists and the positive descriptive words such as *pristine* and strong verbs such as *showcases*.

TUESDAY
1. a. U.S. State Department Web site
2. All customers must carry government-issued identification with them at all times and may be asked to show identification during boarding.
3. Sentence additions will vary. At the last minute, the harried traveler, loaded down with carry-on luggage, squeezed through the turnstile and rammed his way onto the train.
4. A participle is a verb form used as an adjective. The girls *traveling to Poland* had four suitcases.
5. Tourists in Iceland should be careful when exploring glaciers, volcanic craters, geysers, and other natural attractions. There aren't many warning signs and the serious dangers are complicated by high winds and icy conditions.

WEDNESDAY
1. opinion
2. *trans-*: across; *port*: to carry; *-tion*: noun that has been altered from a process
3. How can I choose between Barcelona, Paris, and Vienna?
4. Opinions will vary. Augustine seems to believe that people need to travel in order to know about and understand the world. Robert Louis Stevenson doesn't care where he goes, he simply enjoys the act of traveling.
5. Explanations will vary.
   a. Passports and visas limit access to different countries and allow governments to track an individual's travels.
   b. Visitors to a foreign country must follow local rules.
   c. In case of emergency friends and family should know a traveler's itinerary.
   d. A tourist who flashes expensive clothing and cash becomes a target for thieves and pickpockets.

THURSDAY
1. Edits may vary, but the sentence needs to be reordered. While fishing from a yacht on his vacation, Sam caught a marlin.
2. indisposed
3. A gazetteer is a geographical dictionary listing information about places around the world.
4. American citizens who travel to Barundi, in the country of Bangladesh, are in danger. Although the security situation has recently stabilized, sudden outbreaks of violence continue to pose a security threat.
5. a. ABZ
   b. Ethiopia
   c. Alma Ata Airport

FRIDAY
1. false   4. false
2. false   5. true
3. true
Lists will vary.

Week 25 (pages 77–79)
MONDAY
1. *reunification*: the act of bringing people or factions together after they have been divided; *subsidies*: grants or gifts of money from a government to a private company, organization, or charity to help it continue to function; *unemployment*: the condition of having no job
2. *bias*—an unfair preference for or dislike of something; a prejudice
3. Opinions will vary. The first statement includes a reference that puts the area in perspective.
4. As Europe's largest economy, and second most populous nation, Germany is a key member of the continent's economic, political, and defense organizations.
5. The proverb is a simile. Interpretations will vary, but should reflect the idea that as lies become widespread they grow bigger and bigger.

TUESDAY
1. beside: next to; besides: in addition to
2. countries'
3. false
4. Sentence combinations will vary. At first a system of entangled barbed wire and later a structure of concrete blocks and steel girders, the Berlin wall separated the city into two parts, restricting free travel, for more than 28 years.
5. Both Kennedy and Reagan addressed a worldwide audience. They both hoped to influence public

opinion against East Germany and the Soviet Union. They both aligned themselves with the German people.

WEDNESDAY
1. Any synonym of *inane* is a correct answer: absurd, ridiculous, idiotic, stupid, or silly.
2. Former President Holtz Koehler lives in the capital city of Germany—Frankfurt.
3. A theme is the message or main idea of a story. It may or may not be stated directly.
4. In just nine words Goethe says that life is short and art is enduring, that it is hard to make judgments, and that opportunities don't last forever.
5. Topic sentences will vary.

THURSDAY
1. The chancellor's love of public speaking helped boost her popularity.
2. Many generations of children have enjoyed the Grimm Brothers' famous tales.
3. An antecedent is the word or group of words to which a pronoun refers or that a pronoun replaces.
4. Germany has made capital investments to transform her formerly backward system with extensive land and undersea cable facilities, satellite systems, and fiber-optic networks.
5. Explanations will vary. The term *die Wende* is used to refer to events in Germany that led up to the German reunification.

FRIDAY
1. Three hundred miles as the crow flies.
2. Elbe, Rhine, Danube
3. Netherlands, Belgium, France, Switzerland, Austria, Czech Republic, Poland, Denmark, North Sea, Baltic Sea
4. Answers will vary. Germany has the largest economy, is the second most populous nation, and borders many European countries.

Week 26 (pages 80–82)
MONDAY
1. An autobiography is the story of a person's life written by that person.
2. Many words are correct.
   continuous—broken
   eventually—immediately
   survive—perish
   persevere—surrender
3. While living in Rocky Ridge, Missouri, Laura Wilder edited and wrote columns for the *Missouri Ruralist*.

4. Responses will vary.
5. Thomas Quiner, Henry & Polly Quiner, Eliza & Peter Ingalls

TUESDAY
1. Responses will vary, but should limit either the scope of pioneer experiences or generations.
2. *Laura and Almanzo* is the complete subject, all other words should be underlined. The simple predicate is *struggled.*
3. Sentence combinations may vary. Laura's sister Mary suffered a stroke at the age of 15 and as a result, she lost her eyesight.
4. *Homesteading* means to acquire or settle on land as a result of a homestead law which authorized the sale of public lands.
5. resourceful, persistent, enduring

WEDNESDAY
1. Laura Elizabeth Ingalls was born February 7, 1867, the second daughter of Charles and Caroline Ingalls, in the big woods, seven miles north of Pepin, Wisconsin.
2. uncomplicated, manageable
3. true
4. When they stop farming, Laura and her husband Almanzo will take care of a pet bulldog, a Rocky Mountain burro, and milk goats.
5. Responses will vary.

THURSDAY
1. Writing will vary.
2. A glossary is a listing of important terms used in a specific book or article. It is arranged alphabetically and is usually located at the end of a book or article.
3. Wilder, Laura Ingalls. *Little House on the Prairie* (HarperCollins, 1935).
4. a. Let; b. could have, passed
5. No, you would be too late.

FRIDAY
1. Descriptions will vary, but students should recognize that Viola was a musician, a frontier mother, shy, but willing to work hard to learn new skills.
2. The place was isolated, probably in a rural area of the West. The time must have been around 1930, during the Depression.
3. Opinions will vary. It is clear that both Laura Ingalls Wilder and Betty Bagley respected and admired their mothers and grew up in hard-working frontier families.
4. A memoir is an account of an event or period emphasizing the narrator's own experience of it. A memoir may be written any time about a period that has come before, but is most

often written when an older author reflects on his or her experience.
5. Descriptions will vary.

Week 27 (pages 83–85)
MONDAY
1. *Instruments* is a plural noun and the second sentence uses the pronoun *it* to reference them. The second sentence should read: *They are widely used to accompany Spanish dancing.*
2. The sentence is written from the first person or author's point of view.
3. mortgage
4. piano—quietly; pitch—the level of a sound in a scale
5. Writing will vary.

TUESDAY
1. The flutist went to Oberlin Music Conservatory to learn to play the oboe.
2. a lot
3. Attributes will vary. Several possible responses: extreme, deliberately offensive expressions of alienation and social discontent, strong beat, raw guitar
4. Research questions will vary.
5. "Face It, Girl, It's Over!"; "Fable of the Rose"; "Babe, I'm Gonna Leave You"; "B Is for Barney"; "Baa, Baa Black Sheep"

WEDNESDAY
1. *Who* should be used instead of *whom*; the adjective phrase describes the subject of the sentence.
2. Many explicit verbs are correct: dash, race, sprint; berate, harangue, dispute
3. A ballad is a narrative song or poem.
4. The phrase is a figure of speech meaning that the person remembers the melody or message.
5. The reviewer believes that the orchestra's presentation used volume and instrumental differences to its advantage, but wasn't particularly precise. Opinions on whether the reviewer liked the concert will vary. His review was lukewarm at best.

THURSDAY
1. Their
2. A music dictionary would include definitions of music terms and brief overviews of specific topics.
3. Sahkira is an artist for whom I have great admiration.
4. Any antonym of *melancholy* is correct. *(cheerful)*
5. Proverbs will vary.

FRIDAY
1. The tone of "Over There" is upbeat and optimistic. Its message is that the Yankees' arrival is imminent, and "they" (the Yankees) will save the day. The tone of "When the *Lusitania* Went Down" is solemn and pessimistic. Its message is: Americans are safe only when protected by Old Glory. The song gives an example of a time when Americans were not safe on a British ship. The lyrics suggest that it's time warfare stopped.
2. "Over There" has a quick tempo and strong beat. "When the *Lusitania* Went Down" is much slower and the phrases are longer. Both songs use repetition: Over there—over there, send the word—send the word; some of us lost a true sweetheart, some of us lost a dear dad, some lost their mother, sisters and brothers, some lost the best friends they had. The phrases in the second song are longer and more flowing, without the "punch" of the short, quick tempo.
3. The historical note about the Germans' warfare campaign to attack any ship taking goods to Allied countries contradicted the international agreement to search non-military ships before attacking them. While the lyrics of the song do not place the blame on the Germans for attacking the *Lusitania*, but on those who ignored the warning (the February announcement), it is clear that the songwriter's belief that something had to be done to intervene in the situation (It's time they were stopping this warfare if women and children must drown.) paralleled public opinion in the United States. Writing will vary.

Week 28 (pages 86–88)
MONDAY
1. The home of the Boston Red Sox is a ballpark known as Fenway.
2. metaphor
3. really
4. *foul*—a ball that is hit so as to land outside a foul line; *strike*—a pitch in baseball that is swung at and missed or is in the strike zone and not hit; *bullpen*—the part of a baseball field where the relief pitchers warm up, or the group of a team's relief pitchers; *pitch*—to throw a ball from the mound to the batter

5. The paragraph, written to Red Sox baseball enthusiasts who might visit Fenway park, is meant to encourage a visit. The reference to The Kid, Yaz, and the Green Monster require knowledge of Red Sox lore in order to understand the "pitch". Opinions on the effectiveness of the ad will vary.

TUESDAY
1. Green and red lights on Fenway's manual scoreboard signal balls, strikes, and outs.
2. redsox.mlb.com
3. A red seat in the right field bleachers marks the spot where Ted Williams' homerun, the longest measurable one ever hit inside Fenway Park, landed.
4. Titles will vary.
5. Descriptions will vary. Check to see that the author has made it clear why the player described is an unlikely professional.

WEDNESDAY
1. Babe Ruth, the famous homerun slugger, was a Boston Red Sox player.
2. base runners' cleats, coaches' signals
3. Antonyms may vary. One correct suggestion is *failure.*
4. The room is compared to an autograph book. Its signed walls become the pages of the book.
5. Student reactions will vary.

THURSDAY
1. decision
2. The spirits of legendary heroes linger in the Fenway Park dugout.
3. An index is a list of information or items found in a book, magazine, or other publication. It is generally located at the end of the resource. The information is listed alphabetically.
4. The Green Monster is 20 feet higher than the center field fence and 32–34 feet higher than the right field fence. The screen on top of the Green Monster adds 23 feet, making the wall + screen 43 feet higher than the center field fence, and 55–57 feet higher than the right field fence.
5. The owner of the Boston Red Sox named the ballpark Fenway because it was located in the area of Boston known as the Fens.

FRIDAY
1. upper bleachers–$12; extended dugout box—$260; right field roof box—$45
2. Opinions will vary.

125

ANSWER KEY

3. sections 34, 35, 36, 37, 38, 39, 40, and possibly 41, 42, and 43 depending on seat location
4. $162.00
Directions will vary.

Week 29 (pages 89–91)
MONDAY
1. John Steinbeck's mother, a former schoolteacher, fostered his love of reading and the written word.
2. An inference involves using your reason and experience to come up with an idea based on what a writer implies or suggests, but does not directly state. Making a prediction, drawing a conclusion, and making a generalization are all examples of inference.
3. Steinbeck personifies the hills, giving them the human ability to hug and the human ability to feel jealousy.
4. When something dissipates, it fades or disappears.
5. Students should recognize that the odd jobs Steinbeck held gave him a firsthand look at the farm laborer's desperate working and living conditions. The observations helped Steinbeck develop the themes and plots of many of his major works. The terrain of his northern California surroundings also inspired Steinbeck.

TUESDAY
1. Compassion is sympathy for the suffering of others, often including a desire to help. An author can show compassion in many ways. The tone of a piece and its truthful description are just two possibilities.
2. scrambled, floundered, plunged
3. John Steinbeck, I think, is an interesting man.
4. Student explanations will vary.
5. Student opinions will vary.

WEDNESDAY
1. Student metaphors will vary.
2. bad
3. Steinbeck pursued his writing career in New York but was unsuccessful in getting published.
4. Student opinions will vary.
5. Many examples are possible. War protestors and civil rights activists are two groups that showed their rolling might in the past as they influenced public opinion.

THURSDAY
1. eager
2. During World War II, Steinbeck was a war correspondent for the *New York Herald Tribune*. Once There Was a War, published in 1958, is a collection of some of his dispatches.
3. A coordinating conjunction joins words or groups of words that have equal grammatical weight in a sentence. *And*, *but*, *or*, *so*, *nor*, *for*, and *yet* are coordinating conjunctions.
4. Museum Store
   The National Steinbeck Center
   One Main Street
   Old Town Salinas, CA
5. Student descriptions will vary. Check to see that the descriptions reflect the personality of the vehicle.

FRIDAY
1. b. Steinbeck compares progress to destruction saying that they often look alike. Does he see progress as negative because it tears down or is it positive because it destroys present eyesores?
   c. The moisture-laden air becomes gray flannel that envelopes the Salinas Valley, and the valley is a closed pot with the fog as its lid.
2. Students' words will vary. Steinbeck believed that mankind's most important asset is an exploring mind that is free to take any direction that it chooses.
3. Personal examples will vary.
4. The sky's the limit on this breakfast order!
5. Student descriptions will vary.

Week 30 (pages 92–94)
MONDAY
1. Explanations will vary.
2. An ancestor is someone from whom a person is directly descended, especially somebody more distant than a grandparent.
3. I meet more relatives at my family reunion, than I ever thought I had.
4. Sentences will vary.
   a. I live with my family in a brick house on a quiet street.
   b. Bahasa Indonesian and Dutch are from the same family of languages.
   c. In *The Godfather* Marlon Brando played the part of the head of the family.
   d. Tigers and leopards are part of the cat family.
5. Webs will vary but should include many different types of families.

TUESDAY
1. A nuclear family is at least two people related to one another by blood, marriage, or adoption who share a common residence.
2. allowance, niece
3. Students' reasons will vary depending on their experiences.

4. A bibliography is a list of books and articles appearing at the end of a book or other text.
5. Student interpretations will vary.

WEDNESDAY
1. Mom, Susan's mother is going to take us to the mall, and then her step-dad will bring us home.
2. Explanations will vary.
3. A sibling is a brother or sister.
4. Comparisons will vary. *As* or *like* should be used in comparisons.
5. Definitions will vary.

THURSDAY
1. Michael will finish the drivers' ed class, and then he can drive Father to work.
2. Titles will vary.
3. A researcher would need to know the incomes of many individuals and the level of education each individual completed.
4. The riddle is a pun because Catsup (a tomato-based product) is used by a talking tomato in place of the phrase "Catch up!"
5. Summaries will vary. A researcher from MIT found that first-born children are more likely to be conformists, while later-borns are more likely to be creative and reject the status quo. He also found that a people tend to have more in common with any randomly chosen person of their own age than with a sibling.

FRIDAY
1. Richard Smith is Caleb's uncle.
2. Opinions will vary. The name Earl is the only recurring one which seems to indicate family names are not important to them.
3. They are deceased.

Week 31 (pages 95–97)
MONDAY
1. Synonyms may vary. *Ancient* means belonging to the distant past. (antique, old)
2. If history is the written story of man, it means that man must have developed the ability to keep records or to write.
3. An artifact is an object made by a human being, especially one that has archaeological or cultural interest. Student suggestions for artifacts that characterize their civilization will vary (perhaps a cell phone, an iPod, and a textbook).
4. Archaeologists have found evidence of primitive, independent farming communities in the Tigris and Euphrates River Valleys, the Nile River Valley, the Indus Valley, and the Huang Ho Valley in China.
5. Summaries will vary.

TUESDAY
1. One of the earliest civilizations grew up in an area that stretched from the eastern shores of the Mediterranean Sea between the Tigris and Euphrates Rivers to the Persian Gulf.
2. Student opinions will vary.
3. Cuneiform is an ancient writing system used by the people of Sumer.
4. The first library, founded by the king of Assyria, contained clay tablets with writing on many subjects.
5. Thesis sentences will vary. The long narrative poem *The Epic of Gilgamesh*, recorded on clay around 2000 B.C., represents the finest literary work of ancient Mesopotamia.

WEDNESDAY
1. achievement
2. A powerful Babylonian king, Hammurabi, created a set of laws, Hammurabi's Code, for his people.
3. fact
4. Student writing will vary.
5. Sentences will vary.

THURSDAY
1. Sentences will vary. The Kush peoples who lived along the Nile River south of Egypt beginning around 2000 B.C. were farmers and miners.
2. were
3. One might say that the ancient Egyptians are best remembered and appreciated for their magnificent pyramids.
4. Words may vary—Greek government, ancient democracies
5. Comparisons will vary, but should reflect the information in the drawings and notes.

FRIDAY
1. Hanging Gardens of Babylon, Temple of Artemis at Ephesus, Statue of Zeus in Olympia, Mausoleum of Halicarnassus, Colossus of Rhodes, Lighthouse at Alexandria, Great Pyramid of Giza
2. tour, journey, adventure, foray, visit
3. Student opinions will vary.
Student writing will vary. Check to see that students have supported their choice.

Week 32 (pages 98–100)
MONDAY
1. A *news article* is a story about an event that has just taken place. A *feature article* is a detailed report on a person, an issue, or an event.

126   © Incentive Publications, Inc., Nashville, TN

An *editorial* is an article in which the author gives an opinion on an important issue.
2. The dateline is the notation at the beginning of a news article that tells when and where the story was written. (Sunday • October 27, 2007)
3. Newspapers often represent trivial occurrences in the same way they report details of earth-shattering events. Student agreement will vary.
4. The literary device used is *alliteration*. The title might mean that the subject of the films is only average.
5. Chandralekha (78), an Indian dancer and choreographer known for her philosophical fusing of the classical *bharata natyam* dance form with martial arts and therapeutic varieties of dance, died on December 30 at her seaside home in the Indian city of Chennai.

TUESDAY
1. A good conclusion to an editorial sums up the argument and spurs readers to action.
2. true
3. "Minute Tool Directs Enormous Drill in Search of Natural Gas." New York Times 11 Jan. 2004: 27.
4. b. While **A** uses a good explicit verb (thronged), **B**'s comparison of the crowd to the size of the third largest city has a greater impact because it is a real number to which the reader can relate.
5. Headlines may vary. Members of the British Left Party Waffle on the Issue of the Falkland Islands; Emergency Squad Aids Victim of Dog Attack; Two Sisters, Apart for 18 Years, Are Reunited at a Checkout Counter

WEDNESDAY
1. Many words are possible: newsagent, newsboy, newsbreak, newscast, newscaster, newsgathering, newsgroup, newsletter, newsmaker, newsman, newsmonger, newspaper, newspeak
2. 3, 1, 2 or 2, 3, 1
3. The line of words at the head of a newspaper story or article, usually printed in large type and giving the gist of the story or article that follows, is the headline.
4. true
5. Metaphors will vary.

THURSDAY
1. The phrase is an infinitive phrase (an infinitive plus any complements and modifiers) used as a predicate nominative.

2. Headlines will vary.
3. Both headlines convey a meaning that is probably not intended. The head is not seeking arms, rather the head of a terrorist group is seeking armaments. Farmer Bill could be an individual who perished in a house fire or the sentence could mean that legislators in the House of Representatives failed to act on a bill dealing with farms.
4. advice
5. Lists will vary.

FRIDAY
1. J. Little is writing to the readers of the *Leadville Post* in an attempt to correct misconceptions about a construction project that his company is managing.
2. Words may vary.
positive connotation: crucial, shared, clarify, "set the record straight," diligent, inaccurate; *negative connotation:* insinuating, "fishing for business," speculating, shameless, overzealous, money-grubbing, botched, misleading, glaring
3. misleading, inaccurate
4. Student opinions will vary. The editorial does cast doubt on George Gray's investigative technique and reporting and supports this doubt with examples.
Student sentences will vary.

Week 33 (pages 101–103)
MONDAY
1. surprises
2. Natural gas is clean burning, has low air exhaust emissions, and a reduced level of smog-producing gases.
3. no
4. In his technological advances, civilized man has sometimes failed to use his basic skills. Man is so busy zipping around in automobiles, he fails to walk.
5. An AFV is a vehicle that uses at least one alternative fuel (AF) .

TUESDAY
1. rushing, hurrying, hastening, quickening
2. The sleek new car—the first she ever owned—was her most prized possession.
3. It is difficult to evaluate alternative fuels because the benefits and problems depend on the vehicles that use the fuel.
4. Student names and lists of attributes will vary.
5. Explanations will vary. Ethanol is a clear, colorless chemical compound

that can be added to gasoline to improve the quality of gasoline.

WEDNESDAY
1. Student opinions will vary.
2. If the fuel economy is reduced that means the output one gets for a unit amount of fuel is lower, so a driver can go fewer miles on a tank of gas. This *disadvantage* must be balanced with the advantages that ethanol brings to the environment.
3. inefficiency, incompetence, inadequacy, wastefulness
4. problems in the auto industry caused by technology
5. Sentences will vary.

THURSDAY
1. "Car and Driver Magazine"; How to Buy a New Car by Jeff Holden; Kelley Blue Book
2. Thanks to the latest electronics, cars can tell you the pressure in each tire, display stock quotes, or give directions to the nearest Italian restaurant.
3. Adjectives will vary.
4. The site includes many sources of information so it probably includes both positive and negative resources on alternative fuels. However, since it is sponsored by the U.S. Department of Energy, which is concerned with conservation of natural resources, it may lean toward a push for alternative fuels.
5. Opinions will vary. The words *attractive* and *improving* are both very positive.

FRIDAY
1. The phrase implies that this hybrid uses the newest technology. It is not a car that would have been around when your grandmother bought her car. It may also imply that the car has characteristics a grandmother would not want, for example speed and acceleration.
2. lustrous exterior; powered by the sun; fully gyrating side mirrors; six resilient and self-repairing wheels handle any surface; highly responsive steering and braking; autopilot for driving; interactive computer system navigates and acts as second set of eyes; SafetySurround Bubble
3. Student responses will vary.
4. Student responses will vary.

Week 34 (pages 104–106)
MONDAY
1. *Endemic* is used to describe a disease occurring within a specific

area, region, or locale. An *epidemic* is an outbreak of a disease that spreads more quickly and more extensively among groups of people than would normally be expected. The two words share the root *demos* meaning *people*.
2. Tamara's absence resulted from a bad case of pneumonia.
3. No, an anecdote is a short personal account of an incident or event.
4. *Bruxism*, most often caused by stress, means clenching your jaw or grinding your teeth. It is not contagious, life-threatening, or caused by a virus. It can be diagnosed.
5. The graph shows how life expectancy increased from 1900 to 1940. The biggest change in mortality is seen if the measure is taken at birth.

TUESDAY
1. Student responses may vary. In this author's opinion: **positive**—under the weather, pale, incapacitated; **negative**—diseased, unwholesome; neutral: unwell, poorly, ailing, laid up, peaked
2. symptom
3. *Insomnia* is the inability to sleep, so if one could sleep, insomnia would not be a problem. The line is funny, because it states such an obvious fact.
4. headache, stomachache, heartache
5. Older white or Asian women with small bones and a family history of osteoporosis have a greater risk of osteoporosis. Women in these risk groups can influence their susceptibility by controlling their diet, increasing physical activity, and not smoking.

WEDNESDAY
1. Sentences will vary.
   a. Marsha visits the sick every Sunday.
   b. When Harriet rides in the back seat, she gets sick to her stomach.
   c. The way he wipes his nose with his shirtsleeve is sick.
2. Many answers are correct. Several possible causes—eyestrain, tension, worry, flu, congested sinuses. Several possible effects— inability to work, need for sleep, poor work, blurred vision, irritability.
3. The first word must be a member of the category or set named by the second word. One possible analogy penicillin : antibiotic :: vanilla : ice cream flavor

ANSWER KEY

4. A contagious disease can be transmitted from one person to another either by direct contact such as touching an infected person, or by indirect contact. Many things are contagious—enthusiasm, desire, dissatisfaction, misery.
5. *Foreshadowing* is the author's use of clues to prepare readers for events that will happen later in a story. The reference to dizzy spells foreshadows some upcoming problem.

THURSDAY
1. According to the WHO, health involves physical, mental, and social well-being. Many see health as only a physical condition. If health is mental and social as well, then individuals interested in their health should cultivate mental and social health as well as physical. The implications could affect insurance coverage and health care costs.
2. All infants should receive the first dose of hepatitis B vaccine soon after they are born, and before they are discharged from the hospital.
3. worse, worst
4. Answers will vary. *Healthy*: robust, fit, hardy, vigorous. *Unhealthy*: weak, sickly, frail, unfit, diseased.
5. The prefix *anti-* means *against*. In the case of antihistamine, *anti-* means to prevent the histamine receptors from reacting to histamines.

FRIDAY
1. A rite of passage is a ritual or occurrence associated with a change of status for an individual.
2. Since chicken pox is extremely contagious, it can result in school absences and high medical costs.
3. The article's purpose is to inform. It will probably be read by parents of children who receive the vaccine or who are questioning the need for vaccination.
4. false
Student writing will vary.
  Thanks to the chicken pox vaccine, the chicken pox rite of passage has largely ended and most children in the United States will never have to face the itchy spots as their parents and grandparents did before them.

Week 35 (pages 107–109)
MONDAY
1. Many answers are possible. One might have the idea that language includes a set of rules that govern the use of the symbols and the way in which they are combined.

2. Many words are possible: television, telemarketing, telecommute, telescope, telepathy, teleport, telegraphy, telegram
3. *Can* indicates the ability to do something. *May* indicates permission to do something or the possibility of doing it.
4. Literal language is simple, straightforward, and free of embellishment. It is the opposite of figurative language, which conveys ideas indirectly.
5. Ms. Nova's article has a negative tone. The word *drone* and the phrase *communicated to* rather than *communicated with* indicate a one-way process. The sentence about the cubicle dweller and manager is almost sarcastic.

TUESDAY
1. Advice will vary.
2. Born in 1847 in Edinburgh, Scotland, Alexander Graham Bell became a pioneer in the field of telecommunications.
3. Telephone comes from the Greek word *tele-*, meaning *from afar*, and *phone*, meaning *voice or voiced sound*.
4. Advances
5. "For centuries, humans have tried to teach animals to communicate like humans," said Michael Darre, an animal science professor at the University of Connecticut. "And now we're getting to the point where we're saying, 'Wait a second! Why don't we learn their language, instead of making them learn ours?'"

WEDNESDAY
1. Just as the vacuum tube and the transistor made possible the early telephone network, the wireless revolution began only after low-cost microprocessors, miniature circuit boards, and digital switching became available.
2. true
3. Many answers are possible: Good Morning! Salutations! Hi there! Greetings! Yo!
4. Responses will vary but should support the idea that it is important to develop dialogue and nonverbal communication carefully so that the reader is able to infer a character's feelings and intentions.
5. rumbles, roars, bellows, snorts Additional words may vary.

THURSDAY
1. Student similes will vary.
2. Many answers are correct:

uttered, whispered, moaned, announced, grumbled, shouted, alleged, and stuttered.
3. Many answers are correct: miscommunication, isolation, concealment, suppression, secret.
4. *plan*: a program set up outlining charges for phone service; *anytime*: cell phone minutes that are not dependent on clock hours (They can be used any time.); *cell*: short for cellular
5. Answers may vary. Three advantages: improves safety, engenders a neighborhood spirit, enables drivers to conduct a social roundtable as they sit in gridlock. Three disadvantages: range is only 300-meters, none except drivers with Carhood equipment may communicate, unwanted calls result.

FRIDAY
1. FOR: access to schedules; ability to look up addresses; make emergency calls; communicate with parents; share changes in plans; pass on information; confirm pick-up plans
  AGAINST: disruptive; unnecessary; unfair; no purpose; tool for cheating; undermining education
2. Rankings may vary: 1. riotous; 2. distracting; 3. troublesome; 4. bothersome; 5. niggling; 6. inconvenient
3. Neither editorial supports its contention with solid facts; both use words with strong connotations to influence readers. Examples of phrases that emotionally color the content are "essentially forbidding," "undermining education," and "banning cell phones".

Week 36 (pages 110–112)
MONDAY
1. envisioned, pair of flushed, expected
2. *Pathos* is sadness or suffering. While a character expresses feelings of pity when he shows pathos, the character would probably be morose and sad. Opinions whether those are qualities desired in a friend will vary.
3. Student experiences will vary.
4. Many answers are correct: comrade, buddy, pal, acquaintance, companion
5. The woman is not fashion conscious, she is wearing a summer dress and tennis shoes with a shapeless cardigan and has shorn white hair. Her best friend is a

seven-year-old. The description of permanently hunched shoulders may indicate a character who is eccentric or in some way mentally handicapped. Certainly there exists a special feeling between the narrator (seven-year-old) and the woman.

TUESDAY
1. Mark Twain said, "Good friends, good books, and a sleepy conscience: this is the ideal life."
2. Titles will vary.
3. a. hoping; b. choice; c. safety
4. Student opinions will vary.
5. Student odes will vary.

WEDNESDAY
1. righteous or conforming to a moral standard
2. *to be* (used as a subject), *to listen* (used as a predicate nominative), *to respond* (used as a predicate nominative)
3. Any word beginning with the letters *gr-* is correct.
4. To Alta,
  Like sunshine on a flower
  May your path ever be,
  And may each future hour
  Bring happiness to thee.
  Your friend, Martha
5. The simile compares the grief of two people to a sea and a river intertwining, fusing, and mingling.

THURSDAY
1. buddies, acquaintances, allies, pals
2. Hypocrisy is the false claim to or pretense of having good principles, beliefs, or feelings. Synonyms are *insincerity*, *pretense*, and *duplicity*.
3. innocent, courteous, sympathetic
4. He is saying that to have made it through life as true friends is not a small thing.
5. The kite represents youth and agility, memories of boyhood pleasures.

FRIDAY
1. a. The poet uses *connected* to show empathy and a continuing relationship.
  b. Experiences will vary.
2. Comparisons will vary.
3. Check to see that students give reasons for their statements.
4. Similes or metaphors should make sense.